BREAKING THE WORK BURNOUT CYCLE

A COMPREHENSIVE GUIDE TO CONQUER JOB EXHAUSTION, IDENTIFY SUSTAINABLE SUCCESS, AND REVITALIZE YOUR CAREER

ERNESTINE MICHELS

CONTENTS

Introduction   9

1. THE PROBLEM OF BURNOUT IN THE
   WORKPLACE   15
   Understanding the Concept of Burnout   16
   The Prevalence of Burnout in the Workplace   18
   Causes of Burnout   20
   Signs and Symptoms of Burnout   22
   The Importance of Early Intervention and
   Prevention   25
   Organizational Factors   26
   Addressing Toxicity in the Workplace   28
   The Cost of Burnout to Organizations   29
   The Role of Colleagues in Identifying Burnout   31
   Benefits of Making a Career Change   32
   Risks of Switching Careers   34
   How to Identify a Fulfilling Career Path   35
   Legal and Ethical Repercussions of Ignoring
   Burnout   36
   Did You Know?   38

2. PERSONALITY AND GENERATIONAL
   DIFFERENCES (AND HOW THEY CAN CAUSE
   WORK BURNOUT)   39
   The Link Between Personality and Generational
   Differences and Burnout   40
   Understanding Personality Types   41
   Why Do You Need to Understand?   42
   Generational Dynamics: How Different Age
   Groups Experience Burnout   43
   Managing Conflict: Personality-Based Strategies   46
   Leadership Styles and the Need to Adapt
   Management Practices for Different Generations   47
   Leveraging the Power of Personality Differences
   for Collective Well-Being   48

The Power of Emotional Intelligence and How to
Enhance Interpersonal Relationships   49
Did You Know?   51

3. THE PATH TO SUCCESS   53
Identifying Goals   54
Creating a Roadmap   55
Challenges and Setbacks as Opportunities for
Growth   57
Taking Calculated Risks   58
Developing Healthy Coping Mechanisms   60
Adopting (and Continually Readopting) a Positive
Mindset   61
No More Negativity Bias for a Positive Mind   62
Redefining Your Meaning of Success   64
The Path of Least Resistance   66
What Is the 5-Step Burnout Resilience Formula?   67
Did You Know?   68

4. STEP 1—EXERCISE   69
The Link Between Exercise and Burnout   70
Exercises to Try   70
Making Time for Exercise   72
Finding the Right Exercise Routine for Your
Lifestyle and Preferences   73
The Value of Starting Small   74
Should You Work Out with a Friend or Join a
Group Class?   75
Team Building Activities   76
How to Make Exercises More Fun   78
Exercise and Obstacles   79
Exercises at Work   81
Creative Workstation Modifications   82
Did You Know?   84

5. STEP 2—GOOD NUTRITION   87
The Link Between Good Nutrition and Burnout   88
Understanding Macronutrients, Micronutrients,
and Antioxidants   89
The Need to Stay Hydrated   91
Meal Planning Tips   92

Portion Control 101   94
The Need to Ditch Unhealthy Eating Habits   96
Caffeine and Alcohol Moderation   97
Mindful Eating   98
Did You Know?   100

6. STEP 3—QUALITY SLEEP   105
The Link Between Work Burnout and Sleep
Deprivation   106
Factors Affecting Quality Sleep   107
The Link Between Work Burnout and Sleep
Deprivation   108
Tools for Sleep Quality Assessment   109
How to Deal With Work-Related Sleep
Disruptors   110
Did You Know?   112

7. STEP 4—MINDFULNESS AND MEDITATION   113
The Link Between Mindfulness and Burnout   114
The Science of Mindfulness   115
How to Use Meditation to Learn About Early
Signs of Burnout   117
Why Should You Use Mindful Breathing
Techniques?   119
Mindfulness in the Digital Age   120
Mindful Self-Compassion, Kindness, and
Self-Care   121
Mindfulness Programs That Organizations
Promote   122
How to Enhance Interpersonal Relationships   124
Did You Know?   126

8. STEP 5—TAKE BREAKS AND DISCONNECT
FROM WORK   127
The Link Between Breaks and Burnout   128
Finding the Right Balance: Short vs. Extended
Breaks   129
Strategies for Effective Time Management to
Facilitate Breaks   131
Disconnecting From Work   132
Barriers to Taking Breaks and Disconnecting   133

Taking Breaks to Prevent Decision Fatigue 135
The Art of Pursuing Creative Breaks 136
What You Need to Know About Restorative
Breaks 137
Did You Know? 138

9. SEEKING PROFESSIONAL HELP 139
The Need to Destigmatize Mental Health Care
(and Promote Help-Seeking Behavior) 140
Benefits of Professional Help 141
Types of Professionals Who Can Help 142
The Process of Seeking Professional Help 143
Additional Ways to Seek Professional Help 145
How to Deal With the Cost of Professional Help 146
Tracking Progress, Visualizing Success, and
Making Adjustments 148
Exploring Therapy Options: Finding the
Right Fit 150
Challenging Stereotypes and Misconceptions
Surrounding Mental Health 151
The Subject of Barriers to Seeking Support for
Mental Health 153
Measuring the Effectiveness of Burnout
Prevention Programs 154
What If You Fall Off the Wagon? 156
Did You Know? 157

10. LIFE AFTER BURNOUT RECOVERY 159
Rediscovering Your Purpose 160
Anti-Burnout Trends in the Modern Workplace 161
Self-Care Rituals and Daily Practices 164
Employee Assistance Programs by Employers 165
Leveraging ASMR 166
The Art of Continuous Learning 168
Using Laughter Therapy 169
The Advantage of a Solo Retreat 171
The Power of Random Acts of Kindness 173
Did You Know? 175

Conclusion   177
Glossary   183
References   189

INTRODUCTION

I used to be a go-getter. I loved my job, was passionate about my career, and had a great work ethic. Approach my colleagues, and in a heartbeat, they'll confirm this: I'm the person who always goes the extra mile.

But lately, things went the opposite direction. I felt oddly exhausted, even after about eight hours of sleep. I started to feel less enthusiastic about work.

It was almost impossible to focus and get anything done. Useless is too harsh a word, but I felt as if I was its embodiment. I had zero clue about what was wrong with me. Of course, I want to recover. But how do I proceed? Nary in my life have I experienced anything like this before.

My primary solution? I consulted with my doctor. (Un)fortunately, they also had no idea what was physically wrong with me.

My case remained a mystery for a while. Only after countless research did I discover I was a victim of mild burnout.

WHAT IS BURNOUT?

Burnout or burnout syndrome refers to unmanaged chronic workplace stress. According to the World Health Organization, it's an occupational phenomenon included in the International Classification of Diseases (or ICD-11) (World Health Organization, 2019).

As defined in ICD-11, it's not solely about being tired or experiencing information overload. Rather, it's linked to factors that influence a person's health status. A person who experiences burnout tends to reach out to health professionals.

Sadly, some health professionals don't recognize the phenomenon as an actual problem, regardless of the fact that **79% of currently employed individuals are dealing with burnout** (Rameer, n.d.).

WHO GETS AFFECTED?

Burnout can affect anyone. It can attack men and women, young and old, and those in different generations: Baby Boomers, Generation X, Generation Y (Millennials), Generation Z, and Generation Alpha.

Plus, if you're one of those employees who work long hours with heavy workloads, you're doomed. It can sneak up on you if you're experiencing a high level of stress or pressure (be it in your personal or professional life).

Here are the common types of people affected:

- **Caregivers:** Juggling multiple responsibilities? It can take its toll on anyone and result in unpreventable exhaustion—both physical and emotional.
- **Health care professionals:** The intense pressure and emotional demands of the job can equate to emotional exhaustion and compassion fatigue.
- **Teachers, educators, and school administrators:** Often, they have a high workload and work long hours. They also deal with challenging students or parents.
- **Entrepreneurs and business owners:** Wanting to handle multiple tasks on your own isn't new to entrepreneurs. But the constant pressure and responsibility of running a business? It can be damaging.
- **Students:** They may have a lot on their plate: academic demands, pressure to perform well, and zero work-life balance.
- **Creatives:** They face tight deadlines, absence of inspiration, and pressure to produce new work. Their path also leads to creative blocks and, yes, burnout.
- **Athletes:** The physical and mental demands of training and competing aren't for the faint of heart. In addition to burnout, it can lead to physical exhaustion and mental fatigue.

- **Unpaid volunteers:** Taking on too much responsibility without getting paid or recognized may be fine for a while. But let it continue for years, and what you have is an unwanted mix of resentment and burnout.

COMMON REACTIONS TO BURNOUT

Over 50% of people are affected by burnout (Smith, 2022). But while the syndrome has caused problems to millions already, I can understand why some victims choose to suffer with it in silence. Unfortunately, if you mention you're burned out to others, they might make you the subject of gaslighting and ridicule.

Here are things said to people with burnout:

- **"It's a personal problem (not organizational)!":** In some cases, organizational factors (like no support, toxic coworkers, a pile of work, and work environments) may even be the major causes.
- **"It's just stress!":** A burned-out individual may get stressed. Meanwhile, a stressed individual may just be stressed and not experience burnout.
- **"It's work-related stress!":** Burnout is a multi-dimensional issue. It's not solely work-related, work martyrdom, or workaholism. It can also be because of caregiving responsibilities, personal and professional relationships, or a combination of stressors in different areas of life.

- **"That, too, shall pass!"**: Burnout does not heal on its own. So crossing your fingers (and hoping it'll pass without intervention) will introduce you to its long-term consequences.
- **"You just need a vacation!"**: Rest is non-negotiable. However, addressing burnout requires a series of approaches (see the 5-Step Burnout Resilience Formula), not just a vacation.

MY OTHER SOLUTION

In addition to consulting with my doctor, I also became part of different Facebook groups. One of these groups consisted of teachers who were also experiencing burnout.

While I was no longer a teacher back then (I was running a small business), I wanted to get a grip on the struggles of teachers. I wanted to know how burnout affected them, too.

I crossed my fingers that becoming part of a like-minded community would somehow help me with it. And luckily, it did!

WHAT THIS BOOK CAN DO FOR YOU

This book is an in-depth guide for every burned-out individual. It's for everyone, and it presents a holistic strategy for tackling the work burnout cycle.

I'll also delve into the integral role of leaders and managers. If they strategize (in transforming workplace culture for the better), burnout won't be a problem anymore.

Here are more things this book can do:

- **Acknowledges the pain of burned-out individuals:** Recognize the emotional, physical, and psychological toll of burnout. It can help you make the victims of burnout feel seen, heard, and supported and encourage them to find ways to recover.
- **Identifies the root causes of burnout:** I'll point out and elaborate on the underlying factors that contribute to burnout (workload, lack of control, and interpersonal conflicts). This way, you can address issues more effectively.
- **Present modern ways to overcome it:** There are many strategies for overcoming burnout: self-care practices, boundary management around work and personal time, and so on. I'll walk you through each.
- **Tell you about the *5-Step Burnout Resilience Formula*:** We'll discuss a multi-step burnout recovery plan. In detail, I'll expound on each step to help you achieve a burnout-free life.

Let's begin!

1

THE PROBLEM OF BURNOUT IN THE WORKPLACE

"Emotional labor," which is the effort we make to control and change our own emotions, is associated with stress, burnout, and even physical symptoms like an increase in cardiovascular disease.

— SUSAN CAIN

I'm a teacher and an entrepreneur. My issue with burnout began the moment I felt a bit tired of my situation. For all I knew, I just needed something… different, a change. So, after the COVID-19 frenzy, I sold my company.

Because I worked with more freedom than other people, I didn't think burnout would come for me. But I was wrong. Little did I know that burnout—mild burnout—had already crawled into my life.

On the bright side, it made me realize I had to give more importance to my health. I also want to be proactive. I want to help others address and resolve issues with burnout. And through this book, I'll do just that.

In this first chapter, we'll address the concept of burnout (and how it's on the rise). We'll also discuss the cost of burnout to individuals, organizations, and society. Plus, let's look into the organizations that ignore their employees' mental health and its negative impact on their bottom line.

UNDERSTANDING THE CONCEPT OF BURNOUT

Based on research featured in *Psychology Today*, a media organization that focuses on human behavior and psychology, a psychologist named Herbert Freudenberger coined the term burnout. He first mentioned it in 1974 and described it as an exhaustion of a person's physical and mental resources (Ciampi, 2019).

He also mentioned that while it's characterized by a lack of enthusiasm about practically everything, burnout is more than just that. It's not only about not having enough energy, motivation, and passion; it's also about something deeper.

That said, I can categorize burnout into three dimensions:

1. Physical exhaustion or lack of energy: Even the most menial task can feel like it requires a monumental effort. For example, getting out of bed, walking to the bathroom, eating, and drinking may be challenging.

Also described as:

- wearing out
- depletion
- loss of energy
- debilitation
- fatigue

2. Feelings of cynicism, negativity, and disinterest in your job: They lead to low job satisfaction (or total job dissatisfaction) and desire for a change.

Also described as:

- depersonalization
- irritability
- inappropriate or negative attitude toward clients
- withdrawal
- loss of idealism

3. Acknowledgment of professional inefficacy: Admitting you're struggling to keep up with the demands of your job means you know you need improvement.

Also described as:

- reduced personal accomplishment
- reduced productivity or capability
- low morale
- inability to cope

THE PREVALENCE OF BURNOUT IN THE WORKPLACE

In this age, there's a thing called hustle culture. Its alternative name: burnout culture. What once was an unknown concept skyrocketed to popularity in modern society, especially in the realm of work. The idea behind it is that we must constantly push ourselves to do more, work harder, and achieve greater success.

While there's nothing wrong with working hard, the idea of a hustle culture results in an unhealthy work-life balance. Consequently, everyone feels like they must always be on the clock and never take time for rest and rejuvenation. It glorifies overworking and the sacrifice of personal well-being for professional success—something that can perpetuate the cycle of burnout.

Here is some relevant data:

- **The top three factors that drive burnout:** Lack of recognition or support from leadership (31%), unrealistic deadlines and expectations (30%), and consistently working (29%) are the top factors that drive burnout (Deloitte, 2018).
- **Unfortunately, burnout may feel normal to some:** 66% say they skip at least one meal every day because of stress from their workload, and 1 out of 4 employees rarely, or worse, never take all their vacation days (Deloitte, 2018).

- **Women are more susceptible to burnout:** A disadvantage of this is that workplaces may consider men better than women. Plus, those who prefer particular roles report high levels of burnout (Rameer, n.d.).
- **Burnout is associated with neurodegeneration:** Researchers discovered burnout is linked to a degradation in three cognitive functions (Horvat & Tement, 2020):

  ○ executive function
  ○ attention
  ○ memory

- **Generational differences in reasons for burnout:** Baby Boomers, Gen X, and Gen Z state financial difficulties (like insufficient funds for bills) as their number one reason for experiencing burnout. On the other hand, millennials attribute it to a lack of freedom and time (Rameer, n.d.).
- **The Millennial Generation is more prone to burnout:** 84% of Millennials experience burnout. Pre-2020, about 50% of millennials were already burned out, and the number rose to 59% in 2021 (Rameer, n.d.).
- **Personality plays a role:** When you're emotionally exhausted and have high levels of neuroticism (while being low in extraversion), you'll tend to self-isolate when experiencing work-related stress (Kipman et al., 2021).

CAUSES OF BURNOUT

There are many causes of burnout. However, it all boils down to the fact that you pushed aside your wellness. When people prioritize work (over their well-being), they have higher odds of suffering from burnout.

Here's a closer look into the personal and organizational factors that can cause burnout:

- **Feelings of (mental) suffocation:** It brings about a mix of awful feelings: helplessness, frustration, and stress. If people feel like they have little to no control, it's not a mystery that they'll become disengaged and unmotivated.
- **Flawed leadership:** If leadership and management practices are ineffective, your team may feel awry. They may picture themselves as mere "cogs in the machine."
- **Impostor syndrome:** Employees start having doubts about their abilities. Because they feel they can always do better, they work obsessively to keep up.
- **Ineffective communication:** If employees don't feel comfortable communicating with their colleagues, conflicts, disagreements, and low morale enter the scene.
- **Insufficient recognition:** Employee retention rates fall because of this. If your team members feel their presence is unimportant, quiet quitting tends to start.
- **Negativity:** As a rule, it's not good to see the world from a glass-half-empty perspective.

- **No assistance:** The fear of appearing weak or incompetent can lead to extreme exhaustion and, ultimately, burnout.
- **No work-life balance:** If employees feel that they cannot balance their work and personal lives, they may not want to be at work anymore.
- **Perfectionism:** Perfectionists tend to self-criticize (in an unkind manner). They may fixate on past mistakes and end up with overwhelming feelings of guilt, shame, and inadequacy.
- **Prolonged stress:** If stress is prolonged, the immune system is jeopardized.
- **Role ambiguity:** Anyone who doesn't understand their purpose may eventually lose the willingness to work or even do anything.
- **Toxic culture:** A demotivating work culture can consume employees. It can slowly make them lose interest in their jobs and start rage applying.
- **Unclear job progression:** Nothing makes anyone more anxious than the uncertainty of their future.
- **Work overload:** Assigning your team an insurmountable amount of work can overwhelm and discourage them.
- **Zero boundaries:** There is a fine line between personal and professional matters, and every employee needs to be aware of this.
- **Zero job security:** The wellness of employees suffers if they feel they can lose their jobs anytime. Endgame: a whopping decrease in motivation and productivity!

SIGNS AND SYMPTOMS OF BURNOUT

Burnout is multifaceted, and it manifests in different ways for different people. It's why you need to recognize that everyone has a defining set of circumstances. It's also why there is no one-size-fits-all approach to treating the problem.

Let's discuss the signs and symptoms below.

- **Avoiding responsibilities:** Avoiding work or other responsibilities is a tip to distance yourself from stress and negative feelings. But the things you avoid can add up and bring more problems in the future.
- **Binge eating:** Food can be a source of comfort for some people, and turning to food to cope with stress or negative emotions can lead to unhealthy eating habits, contributing to weight gain and diminished well-being.
- **Compulsive shopping:** Spending money can temporarily distract from negative feelings or stress. But while they can help, they also result in financial problems and more stress in the long run.
- **Declining invitations:** Turning down invitations to events or activities you'd normally enjoy? Then you're withdrawing, potentially isolating yourself, and missing out on valuable social connections and experiences that can enhance your overall well-being and happiness.
- **Decreased engagement with loved ones:** If you're not engaging with loved ones as much as you used to, your fire may no longer be there, and it could be a sign of emotional detachment or a need for reevaluation and

reconnection to nurture and strengthen your relationships for a more fulfilling and supportive social network.

- **Excessive gaming or online activity:** Spending excessive time on video games or other online activities is a ticket to go far away from reality, neglecting essential responsibilities and social interactions.
- **Excessive use of social media:** Scrolling through social media can be a clever way to avoid dealing with real-life problems and emotions because it offers a temporary escape and distraction from the challenges at hand. However, you need to know that excessive reliance on social media can hinder personal growth.
- **Ignoring phone calls or emails:** Effective communication is important in maintaining healthy relationships and navigating professional responsibilities. If you won't take calls or emails, you may be emotionally drained.
- **Increased alcohol or drug use:** Using substances to cope with stress or escape negative feelings can signify burnout.
- **Isolating yourself:** You are spending more time alone and less time with friends or family, which can be a sign of social withdrawal or a need for introspection.
- **Lack of excitement:** Feeling excited about upcoming events or activities is a sign you're 100% on top of your game. It indicates that you have a positive mindset and a zest for pursuing your goals, embracing new experiences, and making the most out of each opportunity that comes your way.

- **Losing interest in hobbies:** If you no longer find pleasure in activities you once loved, you may feel uneasy—I did. This loss of enjoyment can be disheartening and may indicate a potential shift in your interests, values, or overall wellness.

- **Not attending work-related events:** A disinterest in showing up to work-related events (like networking events or conferences) may hint you're showing signs of withdrawal.

- **Not participating in group activities:** Some people like participating in team meetings or other group activities. If you used to be one of them and now you see a sudden shift in your behavior, you may be burned out.

- **Not pursuing personal goals:** Neglecting personal goals or aspirations means you're overwhelmed or unmotivated, and it can create a sense of stagnation or dissatisfaction in your life. You need to identify the factors contributing to this neglect, whether it's excessive workload, lack of clarity, or fear of failure, and take proactive steps to address them.

- **Oversleeping or sleeping too little:** Changes in sleep patterns can be a sign of a problem. Some people may also use sleep as a way to escape from stress.

- **Risky behaviors:** Engaging in risky behaviors (like reckless driving or unprotected sex) may make you feel like a daredevil, but they're a tell-tale sign you have a problem, which could be burnout.

- **Skipping social events:** You cancel plans with friends or family—and frequently, at that.

- **Sleep disturbances:** If someone doesn't get enough quality sleep, their bodies have a harder time repairing and renewing themselves.
- **Unhealthy coping mechanisms:** If we're burned out, we may turn to unhealthy coping mechanisms. These behaviors can further jeopardize the immune system.

THE IMPORTANCE OF EARLY INTERVENTION AND PREVENTION

Early intervention and prevention can help individuals identify and address the early signs of burnout before they get worse.

By addressing burnout at an early stage and promoting prevention measures, organizations can avoid the negative impact of burnout on employee health and well-being. As a result, they'll have a more engaged and motivated workforce and, ultimately, a more successful and sustainable organization.

Here are measures they can take:

- **Address issues proactively:** If organizations don't proactively address problems or conflicts in the workplace, they'll escalate. From a solvable problem, they can turn to something unmanageable and cause serious harm to the individuals or the organization.
- **Encourage open communication:** Creating a safe and supportive environment is important. It should be a workplace where everyone feels comfortable sharing their concerns.

- **Encourage breaks and time off:** Taking regular breaks and using vacation time are simple measures. They're what you can do to prevent burnout from prolonged work periods.
- **Encourage self-care:** Healthy lifestyle habits (like regular exercise, healthy eating, and adequate sleep) can work wonders. Also, promote stress management techniques (like mindfulness or meditation).
- **Follow up and monitor progress:** Consistently communicate with employees and inquire about their well-being to cultivate a nurturing workplace environment, prioritize employee welfare, and proactively recognize indicators of burnout.
- **Foster a positive workplace culture:** Promote a culture of well-being and work-life balance. It's where employees should feel supported in their personal and professional growth.
- **Provide education and resources:** They can offer information about available support services (like counseling, coaching, or employee assistance programs).
- **Recognize early warning signs:** They can keep a vigilant watch for changes—even slight ones—in behavior, mood, or performance that may signify an underlying issue.

ORGANIZATIONAL FACTORS

Organizational factors refer to the elements that shape the culture, structure, and processes of an organization. These factors can tell if you will succeed or fail.

Of course, there are other factors in play. Factors like company values, employee attitudes, and leadership style can also affect the effectiveness of an organization.

Let's look into these factors:

- **Insufficient support and resources:** Becoming frustrated and unmotivated to do the job are realistic outcomes if an employee isn't equipped with the right tools.
- **Micromanagement:** This is the case when higher-ups feel the need to watch closely over everything that employees do.
- **Poor communication and relationships with coworkers and supervisors:** When employees don't feel comfortable communicating with their colleagues or bosses, misunderstandings, conflicts, and low morale enter the scene. As a result, this causes productivity and overall business performance to plummet.
- **Resistance to change:** Organizational resistance to change can hinder progress and innovation. When employees and leaders are resistant to adopting new technologies, processes, or strategies, it can result in stagnation and an inability to keep up with evolving market demands.

ADDRESSING TOXICITY IN THE WORKPLACE

Addressing toxicity in the workplace is crucial for maintaining a healthy and productive work environment.

Here are examples of toxic situations at work:

- **Bullying:** Such behavior may involve the use of offensive language, the dissemination of false information, or the act of isolating individuals.
- **Discrimination:** Treating individuals unfairly or differently based on their protected characteristics, such as age, gender, ethnicity, disability, or religion.
- **Disrespectful communication:** Engaging in aggressive or condescending language, interrupting or dismissing others' opinions, or failing to listen actively and empathetically.
- **Gossiping and spreading rumors:** Engaging in negative conversations about coworkers, spreading misinformation, or creating a hostile work environment through malicious talk.
- **Harassment:** Unwanted and unwelcome behavior based on protected characteristics such as gender, race, religion, or sexual orientation. It may involve offensive comments, gestures, or physical contact.
- **Lack of accountability:** Avoiding responsibility for one's actions, blaming others for mistakes, or failing to take ownership and rectify problems can create a toxic work environment and hinder productivity and growth.

- **Micromanagement:** Excessive control and scrutiny over employees' work, lack of trust, and failure to delegate responsibilities, which can lead to stress, demotivation, and reduced productivity.
- **Passive-aggressive behavior:** Indirect expressions of hostility, such as sarcasm, backhanded compliments, or subtle forms of sabotage, instead of addressing issues directly.
- **Toxic competition:** Encouraging unhealthy competition among employees, pitting individuals or teams against each other, and fostering a hostile work environment focused on personal gain rather than collaboration.
- **Undermining and sabotage:** Deliberately undermining the work or efforts of others, withholding information, or sabotaging projects to cause harm or failure.

THE COST OF BURNOUT TO ORGANIZATIONS

Reduced productivity and increased employee turnover are two big consequences that organizations face. An article featured on *Zippia*, a company that democratizes the aspects of job search, acknowledges how businesses lose as much as $300 billion annually because of burnout-related concerns (Mazur, 2023).

Let's elaborate.

- **A+ productivity:** Your team will feel more engaged and productive. They'll crush their productivity goals and put their best foot forward all day, every day!

- **Low absenteeism and turnover rates:** These will decrease the moment employees feel valued and supported.
- **Creative, futuristic, and highly qualified team:** Foster creativity and innovation, and you'll stay ahead of the curve and maintain a competitive edge.
- **Error-free workplace:** When you prioritize well-being, you'll avoid costly errors and accidents. You'll also keep everyone safe and happy.
- **No work-life imbalance:** One look at your team, and you'll see people with happier, healthier lives inside and outside of work.
- **Positive work environment:** A strong culture helps your employees grow both personally and professionally, benefiting your organization in the long run.
- **Increased health care costs:** Burned-out employees may need more days off to address their health concerns.
- **Questionable competitive ability:** Because of burnout's effect on productivity, morale, and more, it can be challenging for burnout employees to feel competent and innovative.

THE ROLE OF COLLEAGUES IN IDENTIFYING BURNOUT

The responsibility of identifying burnout in the workplace is not solely on the individual experiencing it. Colleagues play a chief role in recognizing early warning signs and intervening before it becomes irrevocable.

Here are measures they can take:

- **Advocate for change:** If employees speak up, listen. After all, colleagues can advocate for changes at the organizational level (like workload management or flexible work arrangements) that may prevent future work burnout.
- **Express concern:** Advise employees to show concern. Tell them that if they sense someone is burned out, they should approach the individual in a nonjudgmental way and express their worry about that person's well-being.
- **Help facilitate communication with management:** It's not new for a person to talk about their burnout. But because of the way they communicate, they're often dismissed as whiners. This is where their colleagues enter the picture—facilitate the conversation or provide support during the process.
- **Help prioritize workload:** Let them help the burned-out individual prioritize their workload. While they're at it, tell them to identify any postponable or delegatable tasks.

- **Offer to cover for them:** Colleagues tend to cover for each other by taking on some of their tasks or covering for them while they take a break.
- **Provide positive feedback:** A burned-out employee could use a boost in morale and motivation. Remind their colleagues to provide positive feedback and recognition for someone's accomplishments and contributions.
- **Respect boundaries:** Every employee should respect the individual's boundaries and not push them to do more than they are comfortable with.

BENEFITS OF MAKING A CAREER CHANGE

Changing careers or job crafting can be a hassle, especially if you have settled for more than a year with your current career. It's a notch harder if you already made lifelong friends, like your work, your employer pays you well, and more. However, if your existing career drives you to a state of burnout, you need to make a difficult decision.

First, let's go over the good things that come with change.

- **Broader perspective and knowledge base:** Changing careers expose individuals to different industries, markets, and professional fields. This broadens their perspective and knowledge base. It allows them to gain indispensable lessons from various sectors and apply cross-disciplinary thinking to their work.

- **Expanded network and connections:** This lets individuals expand their professional network, gain access to different resources and opportunities, and tap into a community of like-minded individuals who can offer support, mentorship, and collaboration.
- **Financial opportunities (possible):** Some industries or professions may have higher earning potential or better compensation packages, providing individuals with the opportunity to improve their financial situation and achieve their long-term financial goals.
- **Long-term career growth:** Going from one career to another opens up new avenues for development, specialization, and advancement within a different industry or profession.
- **Personal growth and fulfillment:** With a new career comes an opportunity for personal growth, fulfillment, and purpose-driven work. It allows individuals to pursue their passions, explore new interests, and find greater meaning in their work.
- **Professional development:** Transitioning to a new career often involves acquiring new skills and knowledge. The process of learning and developing in a new field can enhance career prospects and open doors to exciting possibilities.
- **Personal reinvention:** New careers offer a chance for personal reinvention. It can be an empowering experience that allows for personal growth and self-discovery.
- **Pursuit of passion:** Changing careers often stems from a desire to pursue one's passion. Following one's

passion can bring a sense of fulfillment and satisfaction, making the career change worthwhile.

RISKS OF SWITCHING CAREERS

Changing careers isn't all sunshine and rainbows. The idea behind it may be exciting. However, you also need to be ready for some disadvantages.

Here's what you need to think about:

- **Emotional and psychological impact:** A change means being in a different ball game. It requires individuals to navigate unfamiliar territory, adapt to new work environments, and manage the fear of the unknown.
- **Financial considerations:** Changing careers can involve a period of adjustment, which may include a temporary decrease in income or additional expenses.
- **Limited experience:** Switching careers might mean starting from scratch. Individuals may face challenges in convincing employers of their transferable skills and experience, particularly if they lack a track record in the new field.
- **Uncertainty and risk:** It may take time to establish oneself in a new field, build credibility, and secure jobs. Uncertainty about job prospects, stability, and the overall success of the career change can create stress and anxiety.
- **Skill transferability:** Individuals can leverage their existing expertise and abilities to excel in a new field.

Highlighting these transferable skills can enhance their marketability.

HOW TO IDENTIFY A FULFILLING CAREER PATH

Finding a fulfilling career path requires you to engage in a personal and introspective process. You must actively reflect on your values, interests, and skills to determine a path that aligns with your aspirations. It involves exploring various options, conducting research, and seeking guidance to make decisions you won't regret.

What can you do?

- **Assess your risk tolerance:** Consider your willingness to take risks when choosing a career path. Some careers may involve more uncertainty, while others may offer more stability.
- **Assess your skills:** Make a list of your technical and soft skills. Consider your educational background, work experience, and any certifications or training you have. What are you exceptional at? What feels natural?
- **Consider your lifestyle and work preferences:** Are you more comfortable working independently or as part of a team? Do you want a flexible schedule? Or do you prefer a structured approach?
- **Consider your values and priorities:** Consider your personal values and how they align with potential career paths. Assess whether a particular career path

aligns with your values and supports your desired lifestyle.

- **Experiment and gain experience:** Consider internships, part-time jobs, or volunteering opportunities in fields that interest you. It can help you determine if a certain path aligns with your expectations and brings you fulfillment.
- **Experiment with side projects:** Engage in side projects or passion projects that allow you to explore different interests and skills outside of your current job. These projects can also provide a creative outlet.
- **Explore your passions:** Consider your hobbies, interests, and things you are passionate about outside of work. Sometimes, turning a passion into a career can lead to a more fulfilling path.
- **Research career options:** Conduct thorough research on various career options that resonate with you. Look into job descriptions, required qualifications, growth prospects, and work environments.
- **Request feedback:** Talk to people who know you well —friends, family, or colleagues—and ask for their feedback on your strengths, talents, and areas where they see you thrive.

LEGAL AND ETHICAL REPERCUSSIONS OF IGNORING BURNOUT

The legal and ethical repercussions of burnout aren't something to be taken lightly. Legal consequences can include fines, legal fees, and even criminal charges—all of which are disastrous to a business. On the other hand, ethical consequences refer to damages to the company's reputation, loss of customer trust, and even employee morale.

Here are the potential legal and ethical consequences of burnout:

- **Breach of confidentiality:** When employees are burned out, they may be more likely to make mistakes or violate confidentiality agreements. For instance, they may reveal highly sensitive information they were strictly advised not to divulge.
- **Discriminatory practices:** Age, gender, or race can be subjects of discrimination. For example, if someone is older than the other employees, a burned-out colleague may make fun of them.
- **Employee grievances:** These can arise from poor working conditions, lack of communication, discrimination, harassment, or unfair treatment. When they're not addressed (when employees can't voice their concerns), class-action lawsuits are possible.
- **Increased risk of workplace accidents:** When employees are fatigued and stressed, they may be more likely to make mistakes or have accidents on the job.
- **Retention issues:** Keeping talented employees can be a nearly impossible feat if these people are all about "quiet quitting" or silently seeking better opportunities elsewhere without communication or feedback.
- **Violations of labor laws:** Overlooking violations of labor laws (like the failure to provide adequate breaks

or overtime pay) can happen to burned-out higher-ups. The result? Legal action, reputational damage, and more.

DID YOU KNOW?

Did you know that burnout can actually shrink your brain? Yes, you read that right! Prolonged exposure to chronic stress and the relentless demands of modern life can reduce the size of certain brain regions.

Research shows individuals experiencing burnout have a smaller prefrontal cortex (LaMotte, 2022). The prefrontal cortex is the area of the brain responsible for decision-making, problem-solving, and regulating emotions. This startling discovery highlights the deep impact burnout can have on our overall brain health.

But no need to worry. As long as you take steps to combat burnout, the size of your brain will be alright.

2

PERSONALITY AND GENERATIONAL DIFFERENCES (AND HOW THEY CAN CAUSE WORK BURNOUT)

The effect of burnout differs from individual to individual. According to a medically reviewed article featured on *Verywell Mind*, a resource center that supplies information about health and wellness, much of this has to do with their personality and which generation they belong to (Scott, 2020).

Some individuals actively withdraw, isolate themselves, and give up interest in once-enjoyed activities. Meanwhile, others display irritability, toxic productivity, struggle to concentrate, and let their work and relationships suffer.

Different strokes for different folks, right?

In this chapter, we'll talk about that. We'll discuss the impact of burnout on different personality types, generational dynamics, introversion and extraversion, and more.

This way, you can tap into the power of your personality and use it to thrive in an ever-evolving world.

THE LINK BETWEEN PERSONALITY AND GENERATIONAL DIFFERENCES AND BURNOUT

Various factors, including personality traits and generational differences, can influence burnout. Understanding the link between these factors and burnout is how organizations can effectively address and prevent burnout among their employees.

Here's a closer look at the subject:

- **Career expectations:** Different generations may have varying career expectations. Younger generations may desire rapid advancement and growth opportunities, leading to increased pressure and burnout if those expectations are not met.
- **Technology usage:** Generational differences in technology adoption and usage can impact burnout. Younger generations may experience constant connectivity and pressure to be available, leading to a higher risk of burnout.
- **Work-life balance:** Younger generations, such as Millennials and Gen Z, often prioritize work-life balance and value flexibility. They may be more prone to experiencing burnout if they perceive their work as encroaching on their personal lives.

- **Work values:** Each generation may have different values regarding work, such as purpose, meaningful impact, or work-life integration. When these values are not aligned with the workplace culture, it can contribute to burnout.

UNDERSTANDING PERSONALITY TYPES

You need to explore and understand personality types. Each individual possesses a unique personality that influences their behaviors, preferences, and reactions to various situations.

By delving into the realm of personality types, we can gain indispensable insights into ourselves and others, leading to better self-care practices, effective communication, and a more fulfilling life.

Personality types can be described and analyzed through various frameworks and models, with one of the most popular being the Myers-Briggs Type Indicator (MBTI).

The MBTI categorizes individuals into 16 different personality types based on four key dimensions (Matyanowski, n.d.):

1. **Extraversion (E) vs. Introversion (I):** This dimension describes how individuals derive energy. Extraverts tend to be energized by social interactions and external stimuli, while introverts draw energy from solitude and introspection.
2. **Sensing (S) vs. Intuition (N):** This dimension reflects how individuals perceive and process information.

Sensors focus on concrete details and rely on their five senses, while intuitive personalities are more inclined to perceive patterns, possibilities, and abstract concepts.

3. **Thinking (T) vs. Feeling (F):** This dimension represents the decision-making process. Thinkers make decisions based on logic and objective analysis, whereas feelers prioritize personal values, emotions, and empathy.

4. **Judging (J) vs. Perceiving (P):** This dimension relates to how individuals approach and organize their lives. Judgers tend to prefer structure, planning, and decisiveness, while perceivers are more flexible, spontaneous, and open to new experiences.

WHY DO YOU NEED TO UNDERSTAND?

By understanding your preferences across these dimensions, you can gain insight into your strengths, weaknesses, and how you naturally walk through the world. This self-awareness can help you make conscious choices that align with your personality, leading to a more harmonious and fulfilling life. And when it comes to addressing burnout, knowing your personality type can be particularly helpful.

For example, introverts may need more frequent periods of solitude and quiet to recharge their energy. Meanwhile, extroverts may thrive on social connections and external stimulation. Similarly, understanding whether you lean toward sensing or intuition can help you identify whether you need more sensory breaks or opportunities for imaginative thinking to prevent burnout.

Learning whether your decision-making style is thinking or feeling can guide you in setting boundaries and making choices that honor your personal values and emotional well-being. Judging types may benefit from establishing clear routines and prioritizing self-care, while perceiving types can focus on balancing structure with flexibility and spontaneity.

Understanding personality types is not limited to self-aware-ness. It also enhances empathy and communication with others. By accepting the fact that individuals have different ways of perceiving and approaching the world, we can cultivate greater understanding, tolerance, and effective collaboration. By appre-ciating the unique strengths and perspectives of others, we can not only fight off burnout but also build healthier relationships, reduce conflicts, and foster a more supportive environment.

GENERATIONAL DYNAMICS: HOW DIFFERENT AGE GROUPS EXPERIENCE BURNOUT

Because burnout can affect people across different age groups, you need to recognize that different generations may experi-ence and cope with burnout in distinct ways. Generational dynamics play a significant role in shaping our perspectives, values, and expectations, thereby influencing our experiences of work-related stress and burnout.

Below is an overview of the generations involved.

Baby Boomers (Born 1946–1964)

- challenges in adapting to rapidly changing technology and workplace dynamics may contribute to burnout
- characterized as hardworking and driven individuals
- experience burnout from pressure to maintain high productivity, meet demanding deadlines, and balance work and personal life responsibilities

Generation X (Born 1965–1980)

- known for self-reliance, adaptability, and desire for work-life balance
- experience burnout from pressure to prove themselves in competitive work environments while juggling familial responsibilities
- reconciling traditional workplace expectations with evolving work cultures can be challenging

Millennials (Born 1981–1996)

- experience burnout due to unrealistic work expectations, long hours, job instability, and pressure to constantly prove themselves
- value work-life balance, personal fulfillment, and purposeful work
- the prevalence of digital connectivity and blurred work and personal life boundaries contribute to burnout

Generation Z (Born 1997–2012)

- going into adulthood in a laser-fast digital and tech-heavy world
- experience burnout from pressure to succeed, navigate job market uncertainty, and balance work with social and personal lives
- challenges in establishing identity and finding meaningful work in a competitive environment

Generation Alpha (Born 2010 onwards)

- a high level of parental involvement and supervision can add stress and pressure
- digital dependency promotes an almost-on culture and struggles with disconnecting from technology contribute to potential digital overload
- experience academic pressure from a young age, balancing high achievement expectations with extracurricular activities and well-rounded development
- the youngest generation, with experiences still emerging
- uncertain future and early decision-making about education and career paths contribute to burnout

MANAGING CONFLICT: PERSONALITY-BASED STRATEGIES

A study featured in *Business Horizons,* Indiana University's bi-monthly journal, acknowledges how conflicts arise in workplaces; the failure to manage them is a reason burnout occurs. (Gabriel & Aguinis, 2022).

Here are the personality-based conflict management strategies:

- **Analytical thinker:** When addressing conflicts related to burnout with an analytical thinker, provide them with tangible evidence and data that highlights the impact of burnout on productivity, well-being, and overall organizational performance.
- **Diplomatic peacemaker:** Emphasize the importance of maintaining a harmonious and supportive work environment. Acknowledge their concerns about team dynamics and work-life balance.
- **Assertive leader:** When dealing with an assertive leader in the context of burnout-related conflicts, clearly articulate the impact of burnout on employee morale, productivity, and organizational culture.
- **Empathetic listener:** When engaging in conflicts about burnout with an empathetic listener, create a space for open and honest communication. Allow individuals to express their emotions and concerns related to burnout.

LEADERSHIP STYLES AND THE NEED TO ADAPT MANAGEMENT PRACTICES FOR DIFFERENT GENERATIONS

Effective leadership is important in addressing and preventing burnout among employees of different generations. Identifying and understanding the unique characteristics and needs of each generation can help leaders tailor their management practices and leadership styles to create a supportive work environment.

Here are specific leadership styles and strategies:

- **Transformational leadership:** Transformational leaders inspire and motivate their teams by setting a compelling vision and empowering individuals to reach their full potential.
- **Situational leadership:** Situational leaders adapt their leadership style to the specific needs and capabilities of their team members. They understand that different generations require different levels of support and guidance.
- **Coaching leadership:** Coaching leaders focus on developing the potential of each individual by providing guidance, support, and constructive feedback. This leadership style can be effective in managing burnout, particularly among younger generations.
- **Servant leadership:** Servant leaders create a culture of care, empathy, and support. They listen to employees'

concerns, provide resources for self-care, and promote a positive work environment.

LEVERAGING THE POWER OF PERSONALITY DIFFERENCES FOR COLLECTIVE WELL-BEING

Personality differences among individuals can have an impact on the dynamics of a team or organization. Rather than viewing these differences as obstacles, leaders can harness their power to promote collective well-being. By understanding and appreciating diverse personalities, leaders can create a harmonious and inclusive atmosphere that enhances productivity and collaboration.

Here are some key strategies:

- **Encourage effective communication:** Effective communication is vital for understanding and leveraging personality differences. Encourage open and respectful dialogue among team members, where everyone feels comfortable expressing their thoughts and ideas.
- **Promote collaboration and synergy:** Assign tasks and projects that allow individuals to leverage their unique strengths and work together towards shared goals.
- **Provide tailored support and resources:** Some individuals may benefit from clear guidelines and structure, while others may thrive with autonomy and flexibility.

- **Value diversity:** Leaders should actively acknowledge and appreciate the diverse range of personalities within their team or organization. Each personality type brings unique strengths, perspectives, and contributions to the table.

THE POWER OF EMOTIONAL INTELLIGENCE AND HOW TO ENHANCE INTERPERSONAL RELATIONSHIPS

Emotional intelligence (EI) is a critical skill set that holds significant power in enhancing interpersonal relationships and leadership capabilities. Understanding and harnessing emotions—both in ourselves and in others—allows us to navigate social interactions with empathy, awareness, and effectiveness.

Here are things that require high-level emotional intelligence:

- **Career development challenges:** Facing obstacles or limited opportunities for growth, promotion, or skill development can create stress and feelings of stagnation in one's career.
- **Conflict and disagreements:** Interpersonal conflicts, disagreements, or difficult conversations with colleagues, superiors, or clients can create stressful situations that require emotional intelligence to navigate effectively.
- **Difficult clients or customers:** Dealing with demanding, unreasonable, or difficult clients or

customers can lead to stressful interactions that require emotional intelligence to handle professionally and effectively.

- **Ethical dilemmas:** Being confronted with ethical dilemmas or conflicting values in the workplace can lead to considerable stress as individuals struggle to make decisions that align with their personal and professional values.
- **Financial pressures:** Financial concerns such as budget cuts, financial targets, or meeting sales quotas can create stress and pressure to perform well and achieve financial goals.
- **Interpersonal conflicts with superiors:** Strained relationships, clashes of personalities, or conflicting goals with superiors can cause significant stress and tension for employees.
- **Organizational changes:** Restructuring, mergers, downsizing, or other significant changes within an organization can lead to uncertainty, job insecurity, and increased workload, causing stress among employees.
- **Performance reviews:** Performance evaluations or appraisals can induce stress and anxiety as individuals await feedback and assessments of their work performance.
- **Public speaking or presentations:** Delivering presentations, public speaking engagements, or speaking in front of large audiences can be nerve-wracking and stressful for many individuals.
- **Tight deadlines:** When there is a limited amount of time to complete a task or project, individuals may

experience stress due to time constraints and the need to deliver results promptly.

- **Unclear expectations:** When expectations from superiors or clients are ambiguous or constantly changing, individuals may feel stressed and uncertain about meeting those expectations.

DID YOU KNOW?

Did you know that the baby boomer generation holds the highest rate of entrepreneurship among all age groups (in America)? Despite being associated with retirement, baby boomers are defying stereotypes and venturing into the world of entrepreneurship in record numbers.

Research shows they are starting businesses at a higher rate compared to younger generations. With their wealth of experience, extensive networks, and a desire for continued fulfillment, baby boomers are launching new ventures and pursuing their passions. This trend highlights their resilience, adaptability, and the unquenchable entrepreneurial spirit that defines their generation (Zwilling, 2022).

3

THE PATH TO SUCCESS

Overcoming burnout is an attainable goal. Although it's not for the faint of heart—it requires dedicated effort and psychological capital. It's not something that just happens. Instead, it's something that intentionally happens.

I remember when I worked with a business coach. To help me understand the goal-setting process clearly (and make it less overwhelming), she used a football field (American football) to deliver an analogy.

According to her, the long-term goal is to advance the football to the other side and cross the finish line between the two poles. Meanwhile, the short-term goals involve progressing through the first 10 yards and then the next, and the next.

Throughout these plays, there may be instances where the ball is pushed back a couple of yards or where you have to start over. When it happens, the key is to persist and keep trying. I'm not a big fan of American football, but this analogy stuck with me, and I'll forever remember it.

In this chapter, we'll discuss the importance of setting yourself up for success while addressing burnout. While you may have a burning desire to lead a life free of burnout, you need to acknowledge the challenges involved in treating it.

Moreover, I will introduce you to the *5-Step Burnout Resilience Formula*. By the end of this chapter, I hope you'll feel confident and motivated to take the first step in your personal transformation.

IDENTIFYING GOALS

One of the fundamental steps in combating burnout is to identify and define your long-term and short-term goals. Goal-setting not only provides direction and purpose but also helps you in managing and preventing burnout. By aligning your efforts with your aspirations, you can cultivate a sense of fulfillment and avoid the overwhelming exhaustion that often leads to burnout.

Long-term vs. short-term goals:

Long-term goals:

- help in setting priorities and making strategic decisions
- outline broader objectives and aspirations to be achieved over an extended period
- provide a sense of direction and purpose for the future

- reduce the risk of burnout caused by aimless pursuits or excessive workload
- require consistent effort and commitment to achieve
- serve as a guiding light, keeping you focused on the bigger picture

Short-term goals:

- act as stepping stones toward long-term goals
- allow for flexibility and adjustments based on changing circumstances or priorities
- crush long-term goals into smaller tasks for manageable progress
- encourage celebration of milestones and achievements, preventing burnout by fostering a sense of accomplishment
- help maintain engagement and prevent burnout by avoiding the feeling of being overwhelmed
- provide a sense of immediate progress, motivation, and gratification
- serve as checkpoints for regular evaluation of progress

CREATING A ROADMAP

A roadmap for success serves as a guiding plan that helps you navigate the journey toward your goals. It provides clarity, direction, and a structured approach to maximize your chances of success.

Here are steps that can help you:

- **Define your vision:** What does success mean to you? Clearly articulate your long-term goals and aspirations. Visualize the outcome you desire, whether it's personal, professional, or both.
- **Identify milestones:** Divide your journey into significant milestones that mark your progress. These milestones serve as checkpoints, letting you celebrate achievements along the way and assess your advancement.
- **Develop strategies and action plans:** Determine the strategies and action steps required to reach each milestone.
- **Prioritize tasks:** Assess assignments based on how important and how quickly you need to handle them. Determine which ones require immediate attention and which can be delegated or postponed.
- **Set specific and measurable goals:** Break down your long-term vision into specific, actionable goals. Make them measurable, time-bound, and realistic.
- **Create a timeline:** Establish a timeline that outlines the sequence of tasks and milestones. Consider dependencies and interconnections between tasks.
- **Monitor and evaluate:** Regularly review and assess your progress against the roadmap. Identify potential obstacles or deviations from the plan and make necessary adjustments. Monitoring your journey ensures you stay on track and maintain momentum.

- **Adapt and iterate:** Remain flexible and open to adjustments along the way. Things and situations change, and you need to accept them.
- **Stay motivated and resilient:** Maintain a positive mindset and a strong sense of motivation. Celebrate milestones and achievements to boost morale. Cultivate resilience to overcome setbacks and persevere on your path to success.

CHALLENGES AND SETBACKS AS OPPORTUNITIES FOR GROWTH

Challenges and setbacks are an inevitable part of life's journey, but they also present valuable opportunities for personal and professional growth. Embracing these obstacles with a positive mindset and a willingness to learn can lead to transformative experiences.

Here's what you can do:

- **Cultivate curiosity:** Foster a sense of curiosity and a desire to learn. Approach new situations and tasks with an open mind and a willingness to explore. Ask questions, seek knowledge, and engage in continuous learning.
- **Embrace challenges**: View setbacks and failures as stepping stones toward success rather than as indications of your limitations. Embrace the idea that failure is not permanent and is an essential part of the learning process.

- **Put in the effort and persist:** Understand that effort and perseverance are core factors in achieving success.
- **Embrace constructive criticism:** Instead of becoming defensive or discouraged when receiving constructive criticism, see it as an opportunity for improvement. Develop the ability to separate your self-worth from the feedback you receive and focus on the value it can provide.
- **Emphasize the power of "yet":** Incorporate the word "yet" into your vocabulary. When faced with a challenge or when you haven't achieved a goal, remind yourself that you haven't reached it "yet."
- **Foster a positive mindset:** Cultivate positive self-talk and affirmations. Replace negative thoughts and self-doubt with positive and encouraging statements.
- **Learn from failure:** Don't think of failure as a sign of weakness. Embrace a mindset that mistakes are valuable learning experiences.
- **Understand the difference:** Recognize the distinction between a growth mindset and a fixed mindset. Understand that your abilities and talents are not fixed traits but can be improved with time and effort.

TAKING CALCULATED RISKS

While taking calculated risks can be a catalyst for personal and professional growth, you need to approach them with mindfulness to prevent burnout.

Here are some helpful tips:

- **Consider the risk-reward ratio:** Assess the balance between the potential rewards and the level of risk involved. Evaluate whether the potential gains justify the potential losses or drawbacks. Strive for a risk-reward ratio that aligns with your risk tolerance and long-term aspirations.
- **Conduct a thorough risk assessment:** Evaluate the potential risks and rewards associated with the decision at hand. Consider the likelihood of success, the potential impact on your goals, and any potential pitfalls or challenges that may arise.
- **Manage fear and embrace discomfort:** Taking calculated risks often involves stepping out of your comfort zone and facing fear or uncertainty. Learn to manage fear by acknowledging it, analyzing the potential risks realistically, and focusing on the potential rewards and growth that can come from the risk.
- **Plan for contingencies:** Anticipate potential setbacks or adverse outcomes and develop contingency plans. Identify alternative strategies or exit plans that you can implement if the risk doesn't yield the desired results.
- **Start with small risks:** If you're hesitant or new to taking risks, start with smaller, manageable risks. Gradually expose yourself to larger risks as you gain confidence and experience.
- **Trust your instincts:** While gathering information is crucial, don't disregard your intuition. Gut feelings and

instincts often provide valuable insights that rational analysis may not capture. Trust yourself and your instincts when making calculated risk decisions.

DEVELOPING HEALTHY COPING MECHANISMS

Developing effective strategies for managing and addressing burnout is crucial because it empowers individuals to navigate stress, challenges, and overwhelming circumstances in a productive manner. Burnout often stems from prolonged stress and a lack of effective coping mechanisms, resulting in emotional exhaustion, diminished productivity, and overall wellness decline.

Here's what you can do:

- **Cognitive restructuring:** Identify and challenge negative thought patterns that contribute to stress, replacing them with more positive and realistic perspectives.
- **Practicing gratitude:** Regularly express gratitude by focusing on the positive aspects of your life, which can help shift your mindset and reduce stress.
- **Practicing visualization and manifestation:** Use the power of visualization and positive affirmations to imagine and manifest a future free from stress, fostering a positive mindset and resilience.
- **Progressive muscle relaxation:** Tense and relax each muscle group in your body to release physical tension and promote relaxation.

- **Take up expressive writing:** Write freely and uncensored about your thoughts, feelings, and experiences as a therapeutic practice to release stress and gain insight.
- **Using guided imagery:** Practice visualization techniques by imagining yourself in a peaceful, serene setting to promote relaxation and reduce stress.
- **Using stress balls or fidget toys:** Keep stress balls or fidget toys handy to provide a tactile outlet for stress and help redirect nervous energy.

ADOPTING (AND CONTINUALLY READOPTING) A POSITIVE MINDSET

Adopting (and continually readopting) a positive mindset is an essential component of managing and combating burnout. The way we perceive and interpret the world around us greatly influences our emotional wellness, resilience, and ability to cope with stress. When facing burnout, it becomes even more important to cultivate a positive mindset.

What can you do?

- **Focus on solutions:** When faced with problems or setbacks, shift your focus to finding solutions rather than dwelling on the negatives. Tackle setbacks proactively and do your best to find a solution.
- **Limit exposure to negativity:** Minimize your exposure to negative news, social media, or toxic environments

that can drain your positivity. Choose to consume uplifting and inspiring content instead.

- **Practice acceptance:** Accept that not everything is within your control. Embrace the idea that you can only control your own thoughts, actions, and reactions. Focus on what you can change and let go of what is beyond your control.
- **Practice forgiveness:** Let go of grudges and resentments. Clinging to negative emotions can eat you up inside and hinder your ability to maintain a positive mindset.
- **Positive self-talk your way to anything:** Show compassion and kindness to yourself. Use positive affirmations and inspirational words or statements. Plus, insist on seeing your strengths and previous successes.
- **Reframe challenges as opportunities:** Instead of viewing setbacks and challenges as obstacles, reframe them as opportunities for growth and learning. Seek the lessons and silver linings in difficult situations.

NO MORE NEGATIVITY BIAS FOR A POSITIVE MIND

It can be almost impossible to set yourself up for success and have a positive mind if you think like a pessimist. As much as possible, switch the way you think. The first step is to identify negativity biases.

Here are examples of negativity biases:

- **Catastrophizing:** This refers to exaggerating the negative outcomes or potential dangers of a situation, leading to excessive worry and anxiety.
- **Confirmation bias:** This means you're seeking out information that confirms pre-existing negative beliefs or expectations while disregarding or dismissing information that contradicts them.
- **Dismissing positive experiences:** You're doing this if you're minimizing or discounting positive experiences, dismissing them as insignificant or temporary while dwelling on negative experiences.
- **Dwelling on mistakes:** This refers to ruminating on past mistakes or failures and assigning them more significance than achievements or successes.
- **Emotional amplification:** This is when you amplify negative emotions, such as anger or fear, while minimizing or overlooking positive emotions.
- **Focusing on criticism:** Forget about disapproving compliments. Instead, focus on the good and on the fact that positive feedback is also present.
- **Negating the positive:** This refers to ignoring or downplaying positive aspects of a situation or person, focusing instead on the negatives.
- **Negativity in social comparisons:** You're doing this if you're comparing yourself unfavorably to others and focusing on their achievements, strengths, or advantages, leading to feelings of inadequacy or self-doubt.

- **Overgeneralization:** This is the case of drawing broad negative conclusions based on limited negative experiences, assuming that one negative event or interaction applies to all similar situations.
- **Selective attention:** This is when you pay more attention to negative news, events, or situations while overlooking positive news or aspects of a situation.

REDEFINING YOUR MEANING OF SUCCESS

Redefining your meaning of success lets you align your goals and aspirations with your values and personal fulfillment. It involves moving away from external definitions of success and embracing a more authentic and holistic understanding of what it means to lead a fulfilling life.

Here are steps to help you:

- **Celebrate progress and small victories:** Recognize and celebrate the progress you make along the way. Acknowledge and appreciate the small victories, milestones, and achievements. Appreciate them no matter how insignificant they may seem.
- **Define success through impact and legacy:** Focus on how you can contribute to a greater cause, make a difference in the lives of others, or leave a positive imprint on society.
- **Define success on your own terms:** Take the time to define what success means to you personally. What

experiences, connections, and achievements would make you feel fulfilled and content?

- **Embrace continuous learning and adaptability:** Adopt a mindset of continuous learning and adaptability in an ever-changing world. Success is not fixed or stagnant but a journey of ongoing growth and adaptation.

- **Find balance and prioritize well-roundedness:** Pursue a well-rounded life. Instead of focusing solely on one area, such as career or finances, strive for harmony across multiple dimensions of life.

- **Practice detachment from outcomes:** Know that true success isn't solely defined by external achievements but by your attitude and the meaningful experiences you accumulate along the way.

- **Pursue personal fulfillment:** Shift your focus from external markers of success to personal fulfillment. Prioritize experiences and accomplishments that align with your passions and inner desires.

- **Question societal expectations:** Challenge the societal narratives and external definitions of success that may have influenced your beliefs.

- **Reflect on your values:** Begin by reflecting on your core values and what truly matters to you. Consider the aspects of life that bring you fulfillment and a sense of satisfaction.

THE PATH OF LEAST RESISTANCE

Think of the path of least resistance as a guiding principle that allows individuals to navigate life with greater ease and efficiency. It represents the ability to identify and leverage opportunities where minimal effort is required to achieve desired outcomes. While it may be associated with comfort and convenience, embracing the path of least resistance can also lead to positive outcomes and personal growth.

What to consider:

- **Enhanced adaptability in a changing world:** Choosing the path of least resistance cultivates adaptability, an essential skill in today's rapidly changing world. This adaptability allows for greater resilience and the ability to thrive in dynamic environments.
- **Efficiency and flow:** Opting for the path of least resistance can enhance efficiency and productivity. By identifying the most effective and streamlined approaches, individuals can conserve energy and resources, enabling them to accomplish tasks and goals more effortlessly.
- **Heightened self-confidence:** When individuals choose the path of least resistance and consistently achieve positive results, their self-confidence naturally grows.
- **Positive ripple effect:** By optimizing processes, promoting efficiency, and fostering a positive mindset, individuals inspire and motivate others to do the same.

This creates a supportive environment where everyone can thrive and contribute to a positive and productive collective experience.

- **Simplifying complexity:** Life can often be complex and overwhelming. By choosing the path of least resistance, individuals can simplify their decision-making processes and focus on what truly matters.
- **Sustainable success and long-term growth:** By choosing the path of least resistance, individuals can set themselves up for sustainable success and long-term growth.

WHAT IS THE 5-STEP BURNOUT RESILIENCE FORMULA?

Research says in the face of adversity, misfortune, or frustration, resilience enables us to bounce back. It empowers us to not only survive but also recover and flourish in the aftermath of challenges (Moore, 2019). So if you're burned out, you need resilience more than ever.

Recovering from burnout involves taking these active steps:

- **Exercise:** Engage in regular exercises. The goal is to pacify your anxieties—a 100% body and mind rejuvenation.
- **Good nutrition:** Fuel yourself with nutritious meals. You need to restore vitality and mental clarity.
- **Quality sleep:** Prioritize quality sleep to replenish energy levels and enhance cognitive function.

- **Mindfulness and meditation:** Practice mindfulness and meditation to cultivate inner peace and reduce stress.
- **Take a break from work:** Be intentional about taking breaks from work to recharge and maintain a healthy work-life balance.

DID YOU KNOW?

Did you know that the path to conquering success is far from a straight, predictable line? In fact, it is a journey that often winds through twists, turns, and unexpected detours. While this may initially seem daunting, embracing the unpredictability of this path can actually lead to remarkable opportunities and personal growth.

By accepting and adapting to the challenges and changes that come your way, you open yourself up to new possibilities and unforeseen avenues for success. It is through these unexpected detours that you can uncover hidden talents, learn valuable lessons, and develop the resilience necessary to overcome obstacles.

4

STEP 1—EXERCISE

The power of exercise in combating work burnout is immense—I know it, and most people know it. That's why I commit to starting my day with a 10-minute (or so) stretching ritual.

Stretching helps awaken my body and sets a positive tone for the day ahead. This is a simple yet effective routine that elevates my work performance. It lets me handle tasks and face the challenges of daily life with a boost of energy, a lively spirit, and a sharp mind.

In this chapter, we'll discuss exercise as the first step of the 5-Step Burnout Resilience Formula. We'll talk about a list of exercises worth trying, the value of starting small, the role of a workout buddy, and more.

This way, you'll have a good understanding of why you need exercise and how you can include it in your daily life.

THE LINK BETWEEN EXERCISE AND BURNOUT

Yes, exercise is an effective strategy for treating burnout. It offers a range of benefits that can help alleviate its symptoms and promote recovery.

Here's a quick rundown of how exercise works for burnout:

- **Boosts resilience and stress tolerance:** Regular exercise can enhance an individual's ability to cope with challenging situations.
- **Distraction and diversion:** Engaging in exercise provides a healthy distraction from work-related stressors. Physical activity serves as a break from the routine and can provide individuals with an opportunity to clear their minds and focus on what's in front of them.
- **Endorphin release:** Exercise stimulates the release of endorphins. These endorphins can soothe feelings commonly caused by burnout.
- **Enhances productivity and focus:** By engaging in physical activity, individuals can experience improved mental clarity, enhanced productivity, and better focus, which can help combat burnout-related brain fog.

EXERCISES TO TRY

One of the best ways to exercise? Do it first thing in the morning to turn it into a fundamental part of your day. Then do it day by day. After all, studies show frequency of exercise is more important than how much you exercise (Berman, 2022). Plus, almost anything that involves physical movements counts as exercise: walking, running around, and doing yard work.

Here's what you can do:

- **Circuit training:** It's a series of exercises that target different muscle groups with minimal rest in between. This form of exercise keeps your heart rate elevated and strengthens you.
- **Cycling:** Whether you prefer outdoor cycling or using a stationary bike, cycling is an excellent low-impact cardiovascular exercise. It strengthens your legs and improves cardiovascular fitness.
- **Dancing:** Dancing is a fun cardiovascular activity. It not only increases your heart rate but also improves coordination, balance, and flexibility.
- **Jumping rope:** Jumping rope is an excellent way to let your heart race. It improves coordination, agility, and cardiovascular fitness, too.
- **Rowing:** Rowing is a total-body workout. It targets your back, shoulders, arms, and legs. It provides a great cardiovascular challenge while building strength.
- **Running:** Running is a time-tested cardiovascular exercise. It gets your heart rate up and engages major muscle groups.
- **Kickboxing:** Kickboxing combines martial arts techniques with cardiovascular exercise. It involves punches, kicks, and other movements that provide a

high-intensity workout while improving cardiovascular fitness.

- **Swimming:** Swimming is a full-body workout. It's gentle on the joints, improves cardiovascular endurance, builds strength, and engages multiple muscle groups.

MAKING TIME FOR EXERCISE

If you don't feel you have time for exercise, try to look for small pockets of time throughout the day that you can use for exercise. It could be during your lunch break, early mornings, or evenings. Even short bursts of physical activity can work wonders for your well-being.

Here are strategies that can help you:

- **Make it non-negotiable:** Prioritize exercise for your physical and mental well-being. Adopt the mindset that it's something you need to do (like eating or sleeping).
- **Schedule it:** Squeeze it into your planner or calendar. Set aside specific time slots dedicated to your workouts and commit to them as you would any other commitment.
- **Go with exercises you enjoy:** Select exercises you genuinely enjoy. When you look forward to your workout, it becomes easier to make time for it. Find activities that bring you pleasure and make them a part of your regular routine.

- **Be flexible and adaptable:** If your schedule is tight, be open to different workout options. Break down your exercise into shorter sessions throughout the day if needed. For example, you can do a 10-minute workout in the morning and another in the evening.
- **Multi-task:** Look for opportunities to combine exercise with other activities. For example, you can listen to a podcast or audiobook while walking or use a stationary bike while watching your favorite TV show.
- **Make it a peer activity:** Involve your family or friends in your exercise routine. Plan active outings or workouts together, such as hiking, biking, or playing sports. This way, you can spend quality time while being active.
- **Be efficient:** Choose workouts that provide maximum benefits in a shorter amount of time.

FINDING THE RIGHT EXERCISE ROUTINE FOR YOUR LIFESTYLE AND PREFERENCES

Looking for an exercise routine that suits your lifestyle and preferences for the long haul is no simple feat. However, because having an exercise routine is one of the best actions against burnout, you need to make it happen.

Below are tips that can help you:

- **Assess your fitness level:** Take into account your current fitness level and any specific considerations or limitations. If you're a beginner or have certain health concerns, it may be beneficial to consult with a fitness professional or health care provider to ensure safe and effective exercise choices.

- **Assess your lifestyle and schedule:** Evaluate your current lifestyle, including work hours, family commitments, and personal obligations. Consider the time you can realistically allocate to exercise and identify any potential barriers or challenges.

- **Identify your fitness goals:** Determine your fitness goals, whether it's improving cardiovascular health, building strength, increasing flexibility, or managing stress. Having clear goals will help guide your exercise choices and provide motivation.

- **Explore different exercise modalities:** Research and explore various exercise modalities such as cardio workouts, strength training, yoga, Pilates, martial arts, or group fitness classes. Experiment with different activities to find the ones that resonate with you the most.

THE VALUE OF STARTING SMALL

Starting small is a strategic approach to ensure sustainable and long-term change. As you consistently achieve your initial goals, you can gradually increase the intensity, duration, or complexity of your exercise routine.

Why start small?

- **Manageable and achievable:** Choose simple, achievable goals that you can accomplish without overwhelming yourself. For example, committing to a 10-minute walk every day can be a great starting point.
- **Build consistency:** Consistency is key to reaping the benefits of exercise. By starting with small steps, you're more likely to maintain a regular exercise routine.
- **Gradual physical adaptation:** Taking small steps gives your body time to adapt to exercise. If you've been inactive for a while due to burnout, diving straight into intense workouts can lead to muscle soreness or injuries.

SHOULD YOU WORK OUT WITH A FRIEND OR JOIN A GROUP CLASS?

Exercise with a buddy or a group. It can significantly enhance your exercise experience and increase your chances of staying motivated and consistent.

Here are its advantages:

- **Boosts accountability:** This mutual commitment keeps you accountable and motivated to stay on track with your fitness goals.
- **Provides social support:** Exercising with others offers social interaction and support. It makes your workouts

livelier as you can engage in conversations, share experiences, and celebrate each other's progress.

- **Encourages friendly competition:** Working out with your colleagues can push you to challenge yourself and perform better. Seeing others around you putting in the effort can inspire you to go the extra mile and achieve new fitness milestones.
- **Expands exercise options:** A workout buddy or a group class introduces you to new exercises and training styles that you might not have considered on your own. This variety keeps your workouts fresh and prevents boredom.
- **Expands your fitness network:** This option introduces you to like-minded individuals who share a passion for health and fitness. This lets you connect with individuals who can provide advice, share knowledge, and offer motivation.
- **Spruces up your workouts:** Group classes often incorporate different exercises, training styles, and equipment. Working out with a partner allows for creative workout ideas, friendly challenges, and shared experiences.

TEAM BUILDING ACTIVITIES

Team building activities are excellent at fighting off burnout. In addition to their benefits, they create a sense of unity and result in a cohesive and motivated workforce.

Here's a list:

- **Icebreaker games and energizers:** The idea is to create a positive work atmosphere. These activities can range from simple name games to interactive exercises that encourage laughter and engagement.
- **Collaborative challenges:** Introduce collaborative challenges that require teamwork, cooperation, and problem-solving. Examples are activities like escape rooms, obstacle courses, or problem-solving exercises.
- **Outdoor team-building activities:** Take advantage of outdoor spaces and organize team-building activities such as scavenger hunts, sports tournaments, or hiking trips. They not only encourage teamwork, but they also provide opportunities for fresh air and physical activity.
- **Creative problem-solving activities:** Engage teams in creative problem-solving activities that require them to think outside the box. Activities like building bridges with limited resources, designing and presenting innovative solutions, or creating artistic projects together.
- **Communication exercises:** Conduct communication exercises to enhance active listening, clarity, and understanding among team members. These exercises may include role-playing scenarios, collaborative storytelling, or communication games that improve interpersonal skills.
- **Volunteer work and community service:** Engage in volunteer work or community service as a team. Some examples include volunteering at a local charity,

organizing a fundraising event, or participating in environmental initiatives.

- **Reflective and goal-setting exercises:** Allocate time for reflective exercises and goal-setting sessions as a team. These activities encourage self-reflection, personal growth, and collective goal alignment.

HOW TO MAKE EXERCISES MORE FUN

Making exercise enjoyable and sustainable is important. It's how you can keep up with a consistent fitness routine.

Here's what you can do:

- **Create an inviting workout environment:** Designate a space for your workouts that is clean, well-lit, and comfortable. Play your favorite music, use colorful workout gear, or add motivational posters or quotes to create an inviting atmosphere.
- **Embrace outdoor workouts:** Take advantage of the great outdoors for your exercise sessions. The connection with nature can enhance enjoyment and make your workouts feel like an adventure.
- **Engage in activities you enjoy:** Find exercises that you genuinely enjoy. When you engage in exercises you love, it won't feel like a chore, and you'll look forward to each session.
- **Mix in entertainment:** Listen to music, audiobooks, or podcasts while exercising, or watch your favorite TV shows or movies during cardio sessions. This not only

distracts you from the effort but also turns exercise into an opportunity for entertainment and relaxation.

- **Reward yourself:** Create a system of rewards, especially for your goals. Rewards provide positive reinforcement and help associate exercise with positive experiences, making it more sustainable in the long run.
- **Track your progress:** Use a fitness app, a journal, or a fitness tracker to record your workouts, track your improvements, and monitor your achievements. Seeing tangible progress can be highly motivating and reinforce your commitment to exercise.

EXERCISE AND OBSTACLES

"Not feeling up to it" and "I'm physically incapable of doing that" are among the reasons that can derail your progress with exercises. The solution? Find your intrinsic motivation!

Reflect on the reasons you need to exercise and connect them with your personal motivations. It could be improving your health, boosting your mood, increasing energy levels, or achieving a specific fitness milestone. Reminding yourself of these reasons can reignite your motivation during challenging times.

What to do:

- **Consult with a professional:** If you have any existing health conditions, consult with a healthcare professional before starting or modifying an exercise program.

- **Seek specialized guidance:** Approach a certified personal trainer or physical therapist. They can assess your physical limitations and create a tailored exercise plan.
- **Go with low-impact exercises:** Have joint issues or mobility limitations? Then, consider swimming, cycling, or using an elliptical machine. The idea is to put less stress on the joints while still providing cardiovascular benefits.
- **Focus on strength and flexibility:** In addition to cardiovascular exercise, prioritize strength training and flexibility exercises. They can help support joints, improve stability and range of motion, and reduce muscle imbalances.
- **Listen actively to your body:** Observe any pain or inconvenience. If something doesn't feel right, modify the exercise or consult with a professional. It's important to respect your body's limits and not push through the inconvenience.
- **Modify exercises as needed:** Don't hesitate to modify exercises to suit your specific needs. For example, if you have knee issues, perform squats using a chair for support. Have back problems? Then opt for exercises that involve lying down.

EXERCISES AT WORK

A blog post featured by *Truemark*, a computer software company, says exercising at work is a fantastic way to refresh yourself from feeling burned out (Poudel, 2022). It not only helps you stay physically fit but also enhances mental focus and productivity. While traditional workouts might not be feasible during working hours, there are plenty of fun and unconventional ways to incorporate exercise into your daily routine at work or from home.

Let's explore your options:

- **Active lunch breaks:** Take a brisk walk outside, do a quick workout routine in a nearby park, or even engage in a fun activity like Frisbee or badminton with your coworkers.
- **Deskercises:** Desk exercises are simple yet effective movements you can do right at your desk. Stretching, seated leg raises, shoulder rolls and wrist rotations are a few examples.
- **Desk yoga or stretching breaks:** Look for quick yoga routines or stretching exercises that you can do in a small space. Taking a few minutes to stretch and relax helps release tension and improves focus.
- **Stand-up meetings or workstations:** Implement stand-up meetings or use standing workstations. Standing meetings can be shorter and more dynamic, leading to increased productivity and less sedentary time.

- **Stair climbing:** If your office has a multi-story building, challenge yourself to climb a certain number of flights each day. You can even organize friendly stair-climbing competitions with your coworkers to make it more exciting.
- **Walking meetings:** Walking while discussing ideas or making decisions not only promotes physical activity but also encourages creative thinking.

CREATIVE WORKSTATION MODIFICATIONS

Transform your work environment into a dynamic and health-conscious space, promoting movement, reducing sedentary behavior, and ultimately preventing burnout.

What can you do?

- **Active sitting chairs:** Opt for active sitting chairs (like stability balls or kneeling chairs). They encourage constant micro-movements and engage your core muscles.
- **Adjustable footrests:** Use adjustable footrests to ensure proper leg support and circulation. It reduces fatigue and provides comfort during long periods of sitting.
- **Adjustable monitor stands:** Use adjustable monitor stands to position your screens at eye level. The idea is to prevent neck and shoulder strain and ensure proper ergonomics for a comfortable and productive work setup.

- **Balance tools:** Incorporate balance tools like balance boards or wobble cushions into your workstation, encouraging subtle movements and engaging core muscles while working.
- **Cycling workstations:** Use an under-desk pedal exerciser or a specialized desk that incorporates a cycling mechanism. It enables you to pedal while working.
- **Desk organizers for active work breaks:** Incorporate desk organizers that encourage movement, such as mini stair-steppers or hand exercisers, providing opportunities for brief exercise breaks and increasing blood flow.
- **Desktop document holders:** Position document holders at eye level to reduce strain on your neck and upper back. It results in improved posture and decreased muscle tension.
- **Ergonomic accessories:** Enhance workstations with ergonomic accessories such as mouse pads, ergonomic keyboards, and wrist rests to optimize your posture and reduce strain on your joints.
- **Portable standing desk converters:** Convert your existing desk into a standing desk with a portable standing desk. Not only does this offer flexibility, but it also provides the option to switch between sitting and standing positions.
- **Resistance bands and exercise equipment storage:** Keep resistance bands or small exercise equipment within reach at your workstation. It lets you perform

quick strength-training exercises or stretches throughout the day.

- **Standing desks:** Replace your traditional sitting desk with an adjustable standing desk and alternate between sitting and standing positions throughout the day. This facilitates better posture and increased movement.
- **Standing mat or anti-fatigue mat:** Place a standing mat or anti-fatigue mat in front of your standing desk. It'll cushion and support your feet, relieving pressure and discomfort during prolonged standing periods.
- **Treadmill desks:** Integrate a treadmill into workspaces. It allows you to walk slowly while you work, increase your daily step count, and boosts blood circulation.

DID YOU KNOW?

Did you know that the concept of the aggregation of marginal gains revolutionized the performance of the British cycling team, thanks to the visionary leadership of James Brailsford? By actively aiming for incremental improvements in various areas, the team achieved extraordinary success.

Under Brailsford's guidance, the British cycling team focused on making small yet meaningful improvements in every aspect of their training and performance. They analyzed and optimized factors like nutrition, equipment design, training methods, and even personal hygiene.

The idea is to gain small improvements and just be 1% better at one thing. Each marginal gain may have seemed insignificant on its own, but collectively, they made a remarkable difference.

This commitment to continuous improvement paid off spectacularly. The British cycling team dominated the 2008 and 2012 Olympic Games. The members won numerous gold medals and broke multiple world records.

5

STEP 2—GOOD NUTRITION

I thought I was eating a healthy and balanced diet, but after digging into this subject (after reading and talking with experts), I realized I could do so much more. I noticed that the quality of my work improved after making healthy changes to my meals. I couldn't put my finger on it—I just felt like I was an improved version.

I felt better. I had more knowledge, was more effective at communication, possessed more vital management skills, and showed more empathy.

So in this chapter, that's what I'm going to talk about.

Here, I'll walk you through the second step of the 5-Step Burnout Resilience Formula. As I elaborate on the different discussions related to nutrition, I'll begin by establishing a link between nutrition, work performance, and burnout. Then, we'll dive into macro and micronutrients, antioxidants, how to handle meal planning, caffeine moderation, and more.

The objective of this chapter is to help you incorporate the value of good nutrition. After all, I can attest that if you eat the right food, you'll also feel right and have more energy to fight burnout.

THE LINK BETWEEN GOOD NUTRITION AND BURNOUT

An entry in *Harvard Business Review*, a wholly-owned magazine of Harvard University, reveals that it's no secret that dietary choices can result in burnout (Cross et al., 2020). Sure, eating whatever you want is fine. However, if you want to stay in top shape physically and mentally, be selective about what you eat.

Here's how good nutrition works:

- **Antioxidant protection against oxidative stress:** Burnout can generate oxidative stress, which contributes to cellular damage and exacerbates fatigue. Adding antioxidant-rich foods like fruits and vegetables to your diet provides protection against oxidative stress.
- **Brain health and cognitive function:** Burnout can affect cognitive function, memory, and concentration. Healthy fats (like omega-3 fatty acids) found in foods like avocados and seeds support brain health and enhance cognitive performance.

- **Hydration for optimal function:** Dehydration can worsen fatigue, impair cognitive function, and hinder physical performance. Maintaining proper hydration by drinking enough water throughout the day is key.
- **Nutrient support for stress management:** Burnout is often accompanied by increased stress levels. Nutrient deficiencies can further affect our ability to cope with and recover from stress.
- **Stable blood sugar levels:** Fluctuations in blood sugar? They can worsen feelings of fatigue. You can also include enough protein in your diet to stabilize blood sugar levels.
- **Sustained energy throughout the day:** Burnout often leads to depleted energy reserves. A well-balanced diet, with complex carbohydrates as a key component, provides a steady release of energy.

UNDERSTANDING MACRONUTRIENTS, MICRONUTRIENTS, AND ANTIOXIDANTS

Research says maintaining normal body function and mitigating dysfunction requires a good nutritional status (Muscaritoli, 2021). After all, impaired function often arises from nutritional deficiencies, while consuming recommended levels of nutrients can restore or further improve body functions.

Here's a discussion:

- **B Vitamins:** B vitamins play key roles in energy metabolism, nervous system function, and stress management. Adequate intake of these vitamins through foods can help optimize energy production and mental wellness.
- **Carbohydrates:** Consuming complex carbohydrates like whole grains and legumes can provide sustained energy levels throughout the workday.
- **Fats:** Healthy fats found in nuts and oily fish are good for you. They back memory, concentration, and mood, all of which are essential for maintaining productivity and resilience in the workplace.
- **Magnesium:** Magnesium is involved in hundreds of biochemical reactions in the body, including energy production and stress regulation. Consuming magnesium-rich foods can replenish energy levels and reduce the impact of stress on the body.
- **Proteins:** Incorporating adequate protein from sources like lean meats, poultry, fish, and tofu in your meals is good for you. It supports the maintenance and repair of tissues, including those involved in stress management.
- **Vitamin C:** This antioxidant vitamin combats the effects of stress on the body by supporting immune function. Incorporating vitamin C-rich foods like citrus fruits and berries can help with resilience.

THE NEED TO STAY HYDRATED

If you don't hydrate enough, your energy and focus at work will plummet. When you neglect to drink sufficient water, your body suffers the consequences. Dehydration sets in, draining your energy levels and leaving you feeling fatigued and lethargic.

As a result, your concentration takes a hit, and it becomes harder to stay focused and productive. The effects of not hydrating ripple through your workday, hindering your performance and leaving you feeling less than your best.

Recommended Daily Water Intake

You need to stay hydrated. And while the exact amount of water needed varies from person to person depending on factors like activity level, gender, age, and climate, a general recommendation is about 8 cups every day.

This advice can serve as a starting point, but individual needs may vary. Remember that your body also gets water from other beverages and foods—it's not only about plain water.

Strategies for More Water Consumption at Work

Yes, increasing your water intake can stave off work burnout. Dehydration can exacerbate fatigue, decrease cognitive function, and negatively impact your well-being.

What can you do?

- **Make water easily accessible:** Keep a water bottle or a glass of water within arm's reach at your workspace. When water is readily available, you're more likely to sip on it.
- **Hydration breaks:** Incorporate short hydration breaks into your work routine. Set reminders to take a few minutes every hour to drink a glass of water. It gives you a mental and physical break from work.
- **Opt for water over other beverages:** While it's tempting to rely on caffeinated drinks or sugary beverages to stay alert, they can actually contribute to dehydration and energy crashes.
- **Use a water tracking app:** Use smartphone apps or smartwatch features to track your water intake. These apps can send reminders, provide visual cues, and even gamify the process.
- **Spice it up with infused water:** Does plain water feel monotonous? Then try infusing it with fruit slices or even a splash of citrus. It adds flavor and makes drinking water more entertaining.

MEAL PLANNING TIPS

Implementing a meal planning approach holds immense value. By strategically organizing and preparing meals in advance, individuals can optimize their nutrition, save time, reduce stress, and make healthier food choices. Meal planning empowers individuals to take control of their diet, promote balanced eating habits, and support their wellness.

Here are some tips for you:

- **Adjust as you go:** Life happens, and plans may change. Be flexible with your meal plan and have backup options or simple recipes for busy days or unexpected events.
- **Batch cooking and meal prepping:** Prepare larger portions of meals and store them in individual containers for easy grab-and-go options throughout the week. It saves time and ensures you have nutritious meals readily available.
- **Get creative with leftovers:** Instead of letting leftovers go to waste, repurpose them into new meals or use them for quick and easy lunches. Get creative with ingredient combinations to keep meals interesting.
- **Include a balance of nutrients:** Aim for balanced meals that include a variety of macronutrients (carbohydrates, proteins, and fats), as well as a good mix of fruits, vegetables, and lean proteins.
- **Make a list:** Create a grocery list (using your meals as the basis) with all the ingredients. Stick to the list to avoid impulsive purchases and ensure you have everything you need for your planned meals.
- **Organize:** Keep a meal planning calendar, use meal planning apps, or simply create a visual board to help you stay organized and track your progress.

- **Plan:** Make a list of your meals for the week. Consider your schedule, dietary goals, and preferences. Create a list of recipes or meal ideas for breakfast, lunch, dinner, and snacks.
- **Prep ingredients ahead:** Chop vegetables, marinate meats, or cook grains ahead of time to streamline the cooking process during the week. Not only is this a time-saver, but it also equates to a more efficient meal preparation strategy.

PORTION CONTROL 101

Learning the ropes about portion control can help you maintain a healthy weight. It can also keep the symptoms of burnout at bay. When experiencing burnout, individuals often neglect their physical health, including their eating habits. Practicing portion control can help address this issue by providing structure and balance to one's diet.

Overeating or consuming excessively large portions can lead to feelings of sluggishness and discomfort, which can exacerbate burnout symptoms. On the other hand, properly portioned meals provide the necessary nutrients without overwhelming the body. By fueling the body with the right amounts of food, individuals can optimize their energy levels and enhance their ability to cope with stress.

What can you do?

- **Control snack portions:** Instead of eating directly from the package, portion out snacks into smaller containers or bags to avoid mindlessly overeating.
- **Pack leftovers before eating:** If dining out or ordering takeout, immediately portion and pack away excess food to avoid the temptation of finishing oversized portions.
- **Plan and prep meals:** Planning and preparing meals in advance gives you better control over portion sizes and ingredients compared to eating out.
- **Practice the plate method:** Divide your plate into sections, dedicating half to non-starchy vegetables, a quarter to lean protein, and a quarter to whole grains or starchy vegetables for balanced portion control.
- **Practice the "half plate" rule:** Fill half of your plate with fruits and vegetables to increase fiber intake and naturally control portion sizes of higher-calorie foods.
- **Understand serving sizes:** Familiarize yourself with standard serving sizes for different food groups to gauge appropriate amounts of food.
- **Use measuring tools:** Employ measuring cups, spoons, and a food scale to measure portions when cooking or serving meals at home accurately.
- **Use small utensils:** Using smaller utensils, such as teaspoons or salad forks, can help slow down your eating pace and promote portion control.

- **Use smaller plates and bowls:** Opt for smaller dishware to visually trick your brain into perceiving larger portions, which can help with portion control.

THE NEED TO DITCH UNHEALTHY EATING HABITS

Unhealthy eating patterns can lead to imbalances in blood sugar levels, causing energy crashes and fatigue throughout the day. Consuming excessive amounts of sugary foods and drinks can result in rapid spikes and drops in blood sugar, leaving us feeling drained and less able to cope with stressors.

Besides, it's unquestionable how a poor diet can ruin your mood and mental health. It leads to mental health challenges that can further contribute to burnout.

Here are habits that you need to eliminate:

- **Drinking sugary beverages:** Regularly consuming sugary drinks like soda and sweetened juices can contribute to weight gain and dental problems.
- **Eating fast food regularly:** Frequent consumption of fast food often means excessive intake of unhealthy fats, sodium, and added sugars.
- **Eating in front of screens:** Eating while distracted by screens can lead to mindless eating and overconsumption.
- **Eating large portion sizes:** Consuming oversized portions can lead to calorie overload and weight gain.
- **Eating late at night:** Eating close to bedtime can disrupt sleep patterns and lead to weight gain.

- **Eating processed foods:** Consuming a diet high in processed foods can lead to nutrient deficiencies and an increased risk of chronic diseases.
- **Emotional eating:** Using food as a way to cope with emotions can lead to unhealthy eating patterns and weight gain.
- **Mindless snacking:** Constantly snacking without paying attention to portion sizes can result in excessive calorie intake.
- **Relying on convenience foods:** Depending heavily on pre-packaged meals and snacks can result in a lack of essential nutrients and excess additives.
- **Skipping breakfast:** Skipping breakfast can lead to overeating later in the day and a lack of energy.

CAFFEINE AND ALCOHOL MODERATION

Moderating your consumption of caffeine and alcohol is important. Having too many of these substances may cause you to feel elevated. However, they can lead to problems in your personal and professional life.

Here are some tips to help you:

- **Consider alternatives:** Explore alternatives like herbal teas, decaffeinated options, or natural energy boosters like exercise, proper hydration, and sleep.
- **Keep in mind the rules of moderation:** Know recommended alcohol consumption guidelines. Drinking moderately is equivalent to one drink a day

for adult women, and for adult men, it's up to two drinks a day.

- **Limit intake:** While caffeine can provide a temporary energy boost, excessive consumption can lead to jitteriness, disrupted sleep, and increased anxiety.
- **Pace yourself:** Sip your alcoholic beverages slowly and alternate with non-alcoholic options like water or sparkling water. This helps control the amount consumed and promotes responsible drinking.
- **Plan alcohol-free days:** Designate specific days of the week to abstain from alcohol altogether. This helps break the habit of daily consumption and gives your body time to recover and rehydrate.
- **Observe:** Pay attention to how caffeine and alcohol affect you personally. If you notice negative impacts on your sleep quality, mood, or well-being, it may be a sign to adjust your consumption levels.
- **Strive for a balanced approach:** Prioritize getting enough restful sleep, engaging in regular exercise, and maintaining a nutritious diet. These factors can reduce the need for excessive caffeine or alcohol to cope with fatigue or stress.

MINDFUL EATING

Mindful eating involves bringing awareness and attention to the eating experience. It encourages individuals to slow down, savor each bite, and fully engage with the sensory aspects of eating. While mindful eating is often associated with promoting a healthy relationship with food and weight management, it can also serve as a valuable tool for reducing stress and enhancing work-life balance.

Here's what you can do:

- **Be sharp about your emotions:** Notice any emotional cues or triggers that may influence your eating habits. Are you eating just because you're bored? Mindful eating involves acknowledging these emotions without judgment.
- **Engage in mindful food selection:** When choosing your meals and snacks, consider the nutritional value and how they make you feel. Go with unprocessed foods that provide nourishment to your body.
- **Look into your body's signals:** Develop a deeper connection with your body's hunger and fullness cues. Pause during your meal to check in with how satisfied you feel. This helps you avoid overeating and promotes a more balanced approach to eating.
- **Pay attention to your senses:** Engage all your senses while eating. Be vigilant and observe the smells and tastes of your food. Take small bites and savor each one, focusing on the taste and how it feels in your mouth.
- **Practice gratitude:** Cultivate a sense of gratitude for the food you have in front of you. Reflect on where it came from, the effort put into its preparation, and the nourishment it provides your body.
- **Practice non-judgment and self-compassion:** Approach your eating experiences with kindness and non-judgment. Be gentle with yourself and let go of any

negative thoughts or criticisms related to food choices or eating habits.

- **Reflect on your eating experience:** After each meal, take a moment to reflect on your experience. Notice how mindful eating made you feel, any changes in your level of satisfaction, and how it impacted your well-being.

- **Remove distractions:** Minimize distractions during meals by turning off the TV, putting away electronic devices, and finding a quiet and comfortable space to eat. This allows you to focus solely on your meal and the act of eating.

- **Slow down:** Take your time to eat your meals and chew each bite thoroughly. Slow, deliberate eating allows you to fully experience the flavors, textures, and aromas of your food.

- **Tune in to your body:** Before you eat, check in with your body and assess your hunger and fullness levels. Eat when you are moderately hungry, and stop eating when you feel comfortably full.

DID YOU KNOW?

Did you know that pizza, a beloved comfort food, can offer some surprising benefits when it comes to combating burnout?

The act of sharing and enjoying pizza with colleagues or friends can promote social connection and stress relief, which is vital for preventing and managing burnout. By engaging in light-hearted conversations and laughter over a slice of pizza, individuals can experience a sense of camaraderie and relaxation. Plus, the combination of carbohydrates and protein in pizza can provide an energy boost, fueling the body and brain during demanding periods.

Here's the thing, though: You need to choose healthier pizza options (like those with whole wheat crust, lean protein, and lots of vegetable toppings).

TIME TO RECHARGE

"There is virtue in work and there is virtue in rest. Use both and overlook neither."

— ALAN COHEN

Later in the book, we're going to look at the importance of taking breaks and disconnecting from work... but we're going to start as we mean to go on by taking a break right now.

As you'll see later, taking breaks is crucial to managing stress and preventing burnout, but it has another benefit too: It allows you to consolidate the information you've been taking in, making it much easier to draw on and apply in the future.

So what I'd like you to do now is put the book down, go and make a cup of coffee or pour a glass of water, and move your body a little.

And when you come back before you get back on with the next chapter, I'd like you to take a moment to help other people overcome burnout and workplace stress... I know that sounds like a tall order, but don't panic – you can do that in just a few minutes without even having to leave your house.

You might be surprised to learn that the presence of reviews on a book's listing helps readers who are looking for specific guidance to find what they're looking for.

By leaving a review of this book on Amazon, you'll show new readers exactly where they can find the help they need to break the work burnout cycle.

Simply by sharing how this book has helped you and what readers will find within its pages, you'll show them not only that recovery is possible, but exactly where they can find the information they need to help them get back in control.

Thank you for your support... and now that we've had a sufficient break, it's time to get to the next chapter!

6

STEP 3—QUALITY SLEEP

I prioritize getting a satisfying rest above almost anything else because it's how I'm in top physical and mental shape. Plus, if I'm well-rested, I'm not cranky. I don't snap back at people and end up injuring my personal and professional relationships—the very things I hold dear.

So in this chapter, we'll talk about everything you need to know about sleep. We'll discuss its role in work burnout, the factors that affect quality sleep, what happens if you don't get enough sleep, and more.

This way, you can get to the bottom of your sleep quality and how it can affect your work. If you lack quality sleep, then you'll find the discussions here helpful.

THE LINK BETWEEN WORK BURNOUT AND SLEEP DEPRIVATION

Work burnout is closely intertwined with sleep deprivation. The demanding nature of work, excessive workload, long working hours, toxic colleagues, problematic management, and the constant pressure to meet deadlines can lead to sleep disturbances and insufficient sleep.

Here is a more elaborate discussion:

- **Disrupted sleep patterns:** Individuals experiencing burnout may find it difficult to fall asleep due to racing thoughts, excessive worry, or work-related concerns. They may also experience frequent awakenings during the night, leading to fragmented sleep.
- **Increased sleep disturbances:** Work-related stress can lead to increased physiological arousal and hyperarousal, making it challenging to relax and achieve restorative sleep. Sleep disturbances such as nightmares, night sweats, or vivid dreams may occur more frequently in individuals experiencing work burnout.
- **Insomnia symptoms:** Insomnia, or difficulty falling asleep, staying asleep, or waking up too early, is common among those experiencing burnout. The persistent rumination and stress associated with burnout can add up to the development or exacerbation of insomnia symptoms.

FACTORS AFFECTING QUALITY SLEEP

Everyone knows high sleep quality is important for their health. Sleep experts do not have a universally agreed-upon definition for it. The concept of sleep quality is often subjective and differs among individuals. Rather than having a standardized definition, what constitutes "quality" sleep is often based on personal experiences and preferences (Pacheco & Rehman, 2022).

Here are the factors:

- **Age-related changes:** Sleep patterns naturally change with age. Older adults may experience more fragmented sleep, increased nighttime awakenings, and a shift towards earlier bedtimes.
- **Environmental factors:** Noise, light pollution, and uncomfortable temperatures can disturb sleep. Creating a calm and sleep-friendly bedroom environment can enhance sleep quality.
- **Lifestyle factors:** Factors such as excessive alcohol consumption, irregular exercise routines, and poor diet can affect sleep quality. Maintaining a healthy lifestyle promotes better sleep.
- **Medications and substances:** Some medications, such as certain antidepressants and stimulants, can interfere with sleep. Plus, substances like alcohol and caffeine can mess with sleep patterns.
- **Mental health disorders:** Conditions like anxiety, depression, and insomnia can significantly impact sleep

quality. Addressing underlying mental health issues is necessary for improving sleep.

- **Physical health conditions:** Certain medical conditions like sleep apnea, chronic pain, and respiratory problems can disrupt sleep patterns and reduce sleep quality.
- **Sleep hygiene practices:** Develop a consistent sleep schedule and create a comfortable sleep environment to sleep better. It's also ideal to limit electronic device use before bed and avoid stimulants like caffeine and nicotine close to bedtime.

THE LINK BETWEEN WORK BURNOUT AND SLEEP DEPRIVATION

Combating work burnout requires proactive measures, and one essential aspect is prioritizing and improving the quality of sleep. By implementing the following strategies, individuals can enhance their sleep habits and effectively address work burnout:

- **Avoid stimulants and heavy meals:** Limit the consumption of stimulants such as caffeine and nicotine, especially in the afternoon and evening. Additionally, avoid heavy meals close to bedtime as they can cause discomfort and disrupt sleep.
- **Create a pre-sleep routine:** Develop a relaxing routine before bed to signal your body that it is time to wind down. This may include calming activities like taking a hot shower or watching your favorite movie.

- **Create a sleep-friendly environment:** Design your bedroom to be conducive to sleep. Use blackout curtains and control the room's temperature. Use comfortable bedding and pillows.
- **Establish a consistent sleep routine:** Set a regular sleep schedule by going to bed and waking up at consistent times, even on weekends. The idea is to regulate your internal clock and experience higher sleep quality.
- **Limit electronic device use:** Minimize exposure to electronic devices, such as smartphones, tablets, and laptops, in the hour leading up to bedtime. The blue light emitted by these devices can interfere with the production of melatonin, a hormone necessary for sleep.

TOOLS FOR SLEEP QUALITY ASSESSMENT

Sleep tracking and monitoring tools have gained popularity in recent years as valuable resources for assessing and improving sleep quality. These tools utilize various technologies and methods to track sleep patterns, analyze sleep data, and provide insights into the quality of sleep.

Here's what you need to know:

- **Mobile applications:** Many mobile applications can track sleep patterns. These apps often provide comprehensive sleep reports, sleep efficiency calculations, and personalized recommendations for improving sleep quality.

- **Sleep diaries and questionnaires:** Traditional methods of sleep tracking involve maintaining a sleep diary or completing sleep questionnaires. These self-reported tools capture information on bedtime routines, sleep duration, perceived sleep quality, and factors that may affect sleep, such as caffeine or alcohol consumption.
- **Smart mattresses and sleep monitors:** Smart mattresses and sleep monitors use embedded sensors to monitor and analyze various sleep parameters, including body movements, heart rate, breathing patterns, and snoring.
- **Wearable devices:** Many wearable devices, such as fitness trackers and smartwatches, come equipped with sleep-tracking capabilities. These devices typically use sensors, including accelerometers and heart rate monitors, to collect data on sleep duration, stages, and interruptions.

HOW TO DEAL WITH WORK-RELATED SLEEP DISRUPTORS

Work-related sleep disruptors refer to factors and challenges in the work environment that can negatively impact sleep quality. Acknowledging and effectively managing these sleep disruptors is crucial for maintaining optimal sleep and overall well-being.

Here is something to help you:

- **Environmental factors:** Work environments that are noisy, poorly lit, or uncomfortable can negatively impact sleep quality. Identify and address environmental factors that disrupt sleep, such as excessive noise or inadequate temperature control.
- **Ergonomics and physical comfort:** Uncomfortable workspaces or improper ergonomics can lead to physical discomfort and musculoskeletal issues. Optimizing workstations, using supportive chairs, and incorporating regular movement breaks are practical solutions.
- **High workload and time pressure:** Piles of workload, demanding deadlines, and high-pressure work environments can make it impossible to relax and unwind before bed.
- **Insufficient recovery time:** Take up hobbies that promote recovery and relaxation after work. Incorporating relaxation techniques, engaging in enjoyable leisure activities, and practicing self-care rituals can help individuals unwind, destress, and prepare for restful sleep.
- **Irregular work schedules:** Shift work, irregular work hours, or frequent overtime can disrupt the body's natural sleep-wake cycle. Inconsistent sleep schedules make it difficult to establish a flow that the body can easily follow.
- **Work-related technology and connectivity:** Constant connectivity through smartphones, emails, and work-

related notifications can blur the boundaries between work and personal life.

DID YOU KNOW?

Did you know that our bodies naturally operate on rhythms called ultradian rhythms?

An ultradian rhythm governs our physiological processes, including sleep cycles and periods of alertness. When we neglect this rhythm and push ourselves to the point of exhaustion without taking regular breaks, our productivity and overall well-being can suffer.

7

STEP 4—MINDFULNESS AND MEDITATION

When the COVID-19 pandemic hit, we were quarantined at home. It was fine at the start because I adapted to the safety protocols just fine.

But then, I began feeling like I had too much on my plate. I had so many Zoom meetings, and I had to attend to home responsibilities, too.

I was exhausted, and I suffered remote work fatigue. I realized the only way to move forward was to stop for a while.

I realized if you choose to cancel just one Zoom meeting or postpone a task scheduled for the day, the effect it can have on you is unbelievable. By letting yourself "buy time," you reward yourself with a precious hour that remains unoccupied. More importantly, this grants you the opportunity to take a much-needed break—perhaps go for a leisurely walk or engage in a quick spirit-rejuvenating activity.

In this chapter, I'll walk you through the different things you need to know about mindfulness and meditation. From how it connects to burnout, the science of mindfulness, and breathing techniques to mindfulness in the digital age, mindful self-compassion, and more.

This way, you can make the most of what mindfulness and meditation can do for burnout. If you feel you're burned out, one of the best things you can do for yourself is to refer to the discussions here (along with the discussions in the other chapters dedicated to the *5-Step Burnout Resilience Formula*).

THE LINK BETWEEN MINDFULNESS AND BURNOUT

Saying that the world today is demanding is not an overstatement. And without a doubt, burnout has become such a prevalent issue that it shrouds the perception of almost everyone.

On a related note, mindfulness—a state of present-moment awareness and nonjudgmental acceptance—has gained traction and significant attention as one of the groundbreaking approaches in burnout prevention. And meditation, as a core practice within mindfulness, can cultivate this state of mind.

Below, let's talk more about this:

- **Cultivating compassion:** Mindfulness promotes empathy and compassion, both towards oneself and others. Developing compassion fosters support, understanding, and connection with others.

- **Greater emotional intelligence:** Mindfulness practices heighten your awareness of your emotions and the emotions of others. With this increased emotional intelligence, you can navigate challenging interpersonal dynamics, resolve conflicts more effectively, and build stronger relationships.
- **Prevention of rumination:** Being mindful redirects your attention to the present moment. This interrupts the rumination process and allows you to shift your focus to more positive and constructive thoughts.
- **Restoring energy and vitality:** Regular meditation practice can improve sleep quality and restore energy levels. With moments of relaxation and rejuvenation, mindfulness meditation is how you can recover from the exhaustion associated with burnout.

THE SCIENCE OF MINDFULNESS

Recently, the interest in understanding the science behind mindfulness and its benefits for mental wellness soared. Mindfulness, rooted in ancient contemplative practices, earned a deepening interest in the scientific community because of its promising health effects. Particularly in the context of burnout, meditation practices associated with mindfulness were found effective in mitigating the negative impact of chronic stress and promoting resilience.

Here's a more elaborate discussion on the matter:

- **Cognitive flexibility:** Mindfulness meditation promotes the ability to adapt and shift perspectives. This flexibility helps you reframe stressful situations, think with an out-of-the-box approach, and find alternative solutions to challenges.
- **Cortisol reduction:** Want an easy way to reduce cortisol levels? Then incorporate mindfulness practices. After all, chronic stress can result in elevated levels of cortisol, a hormone associated with stress responses.
- **Gray matter changes:** Studies found that long-term mindfulness practitioners exhibit increased gray matter in brain regions associated with emotion regulation and self-awareness (Tang et al., 2020). These suggest that regular meditation can reshape the brain for the better.
- **Mind-body connection:** Mindfulness practices emphasize the integration of mind and body, recognizing the intricate relationship between psychological and physical well-being.
- **Neuroplasticity:** The brain's capacity for change, known as neuroplasticity, is a key factor in the effectiveness of mindfulness meditation. Regular practice can induce positive changes in neural connections, strengthening circuits associated with stress resilience.
- **Stress response regulation:** The practice activates the prefrontal cortex, which is responsible for executive functions and emotional regulation, and dampens the

amygdala. This neurobiological shift can regulate your emotions and respond more effectively to stressors.

HOW TO USE MEDITATION TO LEARN ABOUT EARLY SIGNS OF BURNOUT

Mindfulness meditation is how you can cultivate mindful awareness, enabling you to identify the subtle signals that indicate the onset of burnout. By developing this heightened awareness, you can take proactive steps to uplevel your situation.

Here's what you can do:

- **Cultivating intentional rest and self-care:** By being attuned to our physical and mental state, we can identify when we require moments of relaxation, leisure, and replenishment.
- **Developing present-moment awareness:** When we direct our attention to the present moment genuinely or without judgment, biases, or attachment to thoughts or emotions, we become aware of our present situation.
- **Enhancing emotional awareness:** Meditation allows us to develop a greater understanding of our emotions and the ability to observe them without immediately reacting.
- **Identifying changes in behavior and energy levels:** Mindful awareness cultivated through meditation allows us to notice changes in our behavior and energy levels. We become more attentive to our motivation,

productivity, and engagement with work or outside activities.

- **Listening to internal cues:** Mindfulness meditation encourages us to listen to our internal cues, such as our intuition and inner wisdom. As a result, we can tune into our own needs, desires, and limits.

- **Noticing changes in sleep patterns:** Sleep disturbances (like difficulties falling asleep, frequent awakenings, or feeling unrested upon waking) often accompany burnout. With mindfulness and meditation, we become more mindful of our sleep patterns and any changes in our quality of sleep.

- **Practicing nonjudgmental self-observation:** Mindfulness meditation fosters a nonjudgmental attitude towards ourselves and our experiences. This self-compassionate perspective enables us to observe our thoughts, emotions, and behaviors without harsh self-criticism.

- **Recognizing thoughts and cognitive patterns:** Through meditation, we learn to observe our thoughts and cognitive patterns without losing ourselves in them. This awareness helps us spot negative thinking patterns, self-criticism, and rumination, which are the most common precursors to burnout.

- **Seeking support and resources:** This lets us know when we need support and to seek help and resources. If we notice early signs of burnout, we can reach out to trusted individuals, such as friends, family, or professionals, who can provide guidance, assistance, and encouragement.

- **Tuning into physical and emotional sensations:** Mindfulness meditation encourages us to observe our physical sensations and emotional experiences with curiosity and nonjudgment.

WHY SHOULD YOU USE MINDFUL BREATHING TECHNIQUES?

Breathing is a core aspect of our existence, and squeezing time for mindful breathing techniques into our daily routines can have a profound impact on our well-being. Mindful breathing involves intentionally directing our attention to the breath, observing its natural rhythm, and using it as an anchor to the present moment. By harnessing the power of breath, we can effectively manage burnout and cultivate a greater sense of calm, balance, and resilience.

What to do:

- **Calming the nervous system:** Mindful breathing activates the parasympathetic nervous system, which is in charge of relaxation and reducing the body's stress response. By consciously slowing down and deepening our breath, we signal to our body that it can relax.
- **Creating mindful transitions:** Incorporating mindful breathing into transitional moments throughout the day can help you navigate transitions with greater ease and minimize burnout.
- **Establishing rituals and boundaries:** You can integrate mindful breathing into daily rituals and

routines. By setting aside dedicated time for deep, conscious breathing exercises, such as morning or evening breathing practices, you're creating a mindful ritual that lets you easily shift from work to rest.

- **Releasing tension and physical stress:** Consciously breathe deeply to release physical tension held in the body. After all, by directing your breath to areas of tension, such as the shoulders or abdomen, you encourage relaxation, alleviate muscle tightness, and reduce the physical symptoms of burnout.

MINDFULNESS IN THE DIGITAL AGE

We live in an age where zoom exhaustion has become an actual problem—where technology blossomed and went on to become an integral part of our daily lives. Inarguably, it introduces us to a plethora of benefits and conveniences and makes our lives so much easier.

However, the excessive use of technology can be detrimental. It can cause burnout and mental exhaustion. The constant influx of information, notifications, emails, and screen time can be heavy on our minds and lead to increased stress levels.

What can you do?

- **Creating tech-free zones and times:** Create intentional spaces and times free from technology. By designating specific areas in our homes, such as bedrooms, kitchens, or dining tables, as tech-free zones, we make opportunities for rest, rejuvenation, and connection with others.

- **Embracing mindful productivity:** The secret is to prioritize meaningful tasks, set attainable goals, and incorporate breaks for mindfulness or physical movement throughout our work or screen time. If we do this, we can optimize our productivity while we reduce the risk of burnout.
- **Engaging in mindful digital consumption:** By curating our digital environments, unfollowing accounts that do not serve us positively, and seeking out meaningful and uplifting content, we can design our digital experiences to nourish us rather than drain our energy.
- **Mindful awareness of digital consumption:** Mindfulness encourages us to bring conscious awareness to our digital consumption habits. By being mindful of the time we spend on screens, the content we engage with, and the emotional impact it has on us, we can make intentional choices about how we use technology.

MINDFUL SELF-COMPASSION, KINDNESS, AND SELF-CARE

In the face of aggravating constant demands, social pressure, and high levels of stress, you need to cultivate mindful self-compassion. Mindful self-compassion involves treating ourselves with kindness, understanding, and care, especially during challenging times.

Here are more discussions about the matter:

- **Cultivating mindful moments of pause:** Create opportunities to step away from the busyness and cultivate self-awareness, allowing us to nurture ourselves amidst the demands of life.
- **Embracing self-acceptance:** Living a mindful life starts with embracing self-acceptance, acknowledging that we are human beings who experience challenges, limitations, and imperfections. All we need to do is practice self-acceptance so we can be free from self-judgment or self-criticism.
- **Practicing gratitude and appreciation:** Mindfulness is also about using the power of gratitude and appreciation for ourselves and our journey. Gratitude also reminds us to focus on the present moment and find joy in the simple things.
- **Recognizing and validating our emotions:** Mindful self-compassion encourages us to know and validate our emotions without judgment. By acknowledging the feelings associated with burnout, we can make a compassionate space within ourselves to process these emotions.

MINDFULNESS PROGRAMS THAT ORGANIZATIONS PROMOTE

Organizations implement mindfulness programs because they know how important it is. They want employees to feel calm and always at ease.

Here are some examples:

- **Active listening seminars:** Training emphasizes the practice of active listening, where representatives give their full attention to the customer and listen without interrupting.
- **Empathy development workshops:** Representatives are taught to empathize with customers by putting themselves in their shoes and acknowledging their emotions and experiences.
- **Mindful language and tone seminars:** Representatives are encouraged to choose their words carefully, use positive and supportive language, and speak in a calm and friendly manner.
- **Nonjudgmental communication workshops:** Training promotes nonjudgmental communication, teaching representatives to suspend judgment and avoid making assumptions about customers.
- **Nonviolent Communication (NVC) training:** NVC workshops are conducted to teach employees the principles and techniques of compassionate communication.
- **Problem-solving mindset training:** Representatives are trained to approach customer issues with a problem-solving mindset. They learn to focus on finding solutions.

HOW TO ENHANCE INTERPERSONAL RELATIONSHIPS

According to an article in Forbes, effective communication is a cornerstone of healthy relationships—both personally and professionally (Attard, 2022). In the face of burnout, cultivating mindful communication can be a powerful tool for enhancing interpersonal connections and reducing the risk of further exhaustion.

Mindful communication is about bringing present-moment awareness, compassion, and intentionality to our interactions with others. By fostering open and authentic dialogue, practicing active listening, and cultivating empathy, we can establish an environment that promotes wellness and prevents burnout.

Here are relevant discussions:

- **Building supportive networks:** By fostering meaningful connections and relationships, we set a support system that can provide understanding, empathy, and guidance. Among many good things, a strong support network helps prevent isolation.
- **Conscious and clear expression:** Mindful communication involves expressing ourselves consciously and clearly. By taking the time to choose our words thoughtfully, we promote effective and respectful communication. We learn to minimize misunderstandings, reduce conflicts, and enhance trust.
- **Conflict resolution:** When we approach conflicts with openness, curiosity, and a willingness to understand

multiple perspectives, we're opening up opportunities for growth, understanding, and resolution.

- **Honoring boundaries:** When we acknowledge other people's limits, we create a sense of safety and trust in our relationships. Honoring boundaries promotes healthy interactions, reduces feelings of overwhelm, and prevents burnout resulting from emotional and energetic depletion.

- **Mindful feedback and appreciation:** By offering constructive feedback with empathy and compassion, we build an environment that encourages progress. Plus, expressing appreciation and gratitude for other people's work and contributions leads to a positive and supportive atmosphere.

- **Nonjudgmental listening:** Instead of jumping to conclusions or formulating responses in our minds, we give our full attention to the speaker, suspending judgment and truly hearing their words. This encourages an open and safe space for expression, deepens trust, and strengthens relationships.

- **Self-reflection and continuous learning:** Mindful communication involves self-reflection and continuous learning. By reflecting on our own communication patterns, strengths, and areas for improvement, we can enhance our interpersonal skills. This self-reflection leads to personal growth and prevents burnout resulting from ineffective or stressful communication dynamics.

DID YOU KNOW?

Did you know about the concept of "monk mode?" It's a meditative work practice. It can supercharge your focus and productivity.

Monk mode involves immersing yourself fully in a single task or project, similar to how monks dedicate themselves to their spiritual practices. By eliminating all distractions and external stimuli, you make a sacred space for deep work and concentration.

During monk mode, you set aside designated blocks of time to focus exclusively on your most important work, free from interruptions. This intense level of concentration allows you to tap into a state of flow where you can accomplish tasks with heightened efficiency and quality.

8

STEP 5—TAKE BREAKS AND DISCONNECT FROM WORK

I remember the time when the World Health Organization proclaimed it was safe to leave the house. Being stuck at home for months meant safety and security from COVID-19.

Without a doubt, a portion of the global population was fascinated with remote work—they thrived in it and became at least twice as productive. However, another portion missed the social component of work. They ended up with "remote work fatigue," missed seeing colleagues, and longed for workplace action.

In this chapter, that's what we'll talk about. Let's go over the need to take breaks and disconnect from work as the final step of the *5-Step Burnout Resilience Formula*. We'll talk about the link between breaks and burnout, the impact of continuous work, strategies for effective breaks, and more.

This way, you'll have all the information you need about the importance of a break. More importantly, getting a strong foundation in this subject will motivate you to apply the 5-Step Burnout Resilience Formula to live a burnout-free life.

THE LINK BETWEEN BREAKS AND BURNOUT

The link between breaks and burnout is a critical aspect to understand and address in the workplace. It's a result of prolonged and unmanaged stress, and the lack of breaks can contribute significantly to this phenomenon.

Here's a highlight of the link between the two:

- **Accumulated stress:** The absence of breaks denies individuals the opportunity to alleviate stress. As a result, the concern worsens to heightened levels of tension and exhaustion.
- **Breaks as prevention and recovery:** Breaks serve as a preventive measure against burnout and aid in its recovery. Intentional breaks throughout the workday allow individuals to recharge, refocus, and manage stress levels effectively.
- **Diminished wellness:** Mental and physical health are closely interconnected, and neglecting breaks can result in different health issues, such as sleep disturbances, increased anxiety, depression, and a weakened immune system.
- **Fatigue and declining performance:** The exhaustion from prolonged work diminishes their focus, attention

span, and problem-solving skills. This decline in performance can lead to feelings of inadequacy and frustration, exacerbating the risk of burnout.

- **Lack of rest and recovery:** Without adequate breaks, individuals are more prone to physical and mental exhaustion, resulting in decreased productivity, impaired concentration, and decreased cognitive functioning.
- **Reduced resilience:** Taking breaks plays a vital role in building resilience against stress and adversity. Over time, you become more vulnerable to burnout if you don't take breaks.

FINDING THE RIGHT BALANCE: SHORT VS. EXTENDED BREAKS

Finding the right balance between short and extended breaks is crucial for optimizing productivity, mental well-being, and overall work performance. Both types of breaks have their advantages and serve different purposes in promoting rest and rejuvenation.

Here's what to consider:

- **Adaptability:** The balance between short and extended breaks is not fixed and may vary based on specific circumstances and work demands. Being flexible and adaptable allows you to adjust your break patterns to meet changing needs.

- **Extended breaks:** They refer to longer periods of time away from work, typically lasting 30 minutes to an hour or more. Activities during extended breaks can include hobbies, exercise, spending time with loved ones, pursuing personal interests, or engaging in activities that bring joy and fulfillment.
- **Experimentation and self-awareness:** Pay attention to how different break durations impact your focus and energy levels. Assess your productivity, mental clarity, and emotional state before and after different types of breaks to determine which approach is the most favorable.
- **Personal preferences and needs:** Some individuals may find that short breaks at regular intervals help them maintain focus and productivity, while others may benefit from longer, uninterrupted periods of downtime. Reflect on your personal work rhythm, energy levels, and how different break durations impact your mental state.
- **Short breaks:** Short breaks typically range from a few minutes to 10 minutes and provide brief moments of respite during work hours. These breaks are valuable for immediate relief and can help combat mental fatigue and enhance focus.
- **Task and time management:** The choice between short and extended breaks depends on the nature of tasks, deadlines, and individual work styles. Assessing the workload and scheduling breaks strategically can help strike the right balance between the two.

STRATEGIES FOR EFFECTIVE TIME MANAGEMENT TO FACILITATE BREAKS

Effective time management is key to facilitating regular breaks and optimizing productivity. By implementing strategies to manage your time more efficiently, you can create dedicated periods for breaks without sacrificing work performance.

Here are strategies to try:

- **Adjust breaks to task demands:** Consider adjusting the frequency and duration of your breaks based on the nature of your tasks. More mentally demanding tasks may require more frequent short breaks, while less intense tasks may allow for longer breaks.
- **Customize break management:** Experiment with different approaches to break management and find what works best for you. Everyone's preferences and needs are unique, so adjust your break routine to suit your individual style and optimize your productivity.
- **Determine break duration:** Decide on the duration of your breaks based on your personal preferences and work requirements. Short, frequent breaks of 5 to 10 minutes every hour or two can help maintain focus, while longer breaks of 15 to 30 minutes every few hours allow for more relaxation and recharge.
- **Move and stretch:** Physical activity during breaks can boost energy levels and refresh your mind. Take a short walk, do some stretching exercises, or engage in light

physical activities to promote blood circulation and alleviate any built-up tension.

- **Time blocking:** Use the technique of time blocking to schedule specific blocks of time for different activities. Assign blocks of time for focused work, meetings, administrative tasks, and breaks.
- **Time-tracking tools:** Monitor and analyze how you spend your time. These tools help you identify patterns, track productivity, and identify areas where time may be wasted or mismanaged. By understanding how you allocate your time, you can make adjustments to ensure that you are utilizing your time efficiently and creating opportunities for breaks.

DISCONNECTING FROM WORK

Disconnecting from work is essential for maintaining a healthy work-life balance and preventing burnout. While traditional methods like taking vacations or practicing mindfulness are effective, there are also unconventional ways to disconnect and recharge.

Here are some unconventional strategies to help you disconnect from work:

- **Adventure and exploration:** Seek out new experiences and adventures to break away from work routines. Take up activities that push you out of your comfort zone: rock climbing, skydiving, or trying a new sport.

- **Artistic expression:** Tap into your creative side as a means of disconnecting. Invest time in painting, drawing, playing a musical instrument, or writing. Artistic expression gives you an outlet for self-expression and can serve as a therapeutic escape from work-related stress.
- **Nature immersion:** Spend time in nature to disconnect from the demands of work. Unplug from technology and immerse yourself in the outdoors. Take hikes, go camping, or simply find a peaceful spot in a park.
- **Sensory experiences:** Have sensory experiences that evoke relaxation and pleasure. Explore aromatherapy, indulge in a soothing bath with essential oils, or savor a delicious meal.
- **Socializing and connection:** Spend quality time with loved ones and friends. Engaging in meaningful conversations and shared activities can provide a sense of connection and joy and help you take your mind off work-related pressures and stressors.

BARRIERS TO TAKING BREAKS AND DISCONNECTING

Taking breaks and disconnecting from work is vital for maintaining wellness and productivity. However, there are barriers that prevent individuals from effectively disconnecting.

Here are the barriers:

- **Difficulty switching off:** It can be challenging to mentally disconnect from work, especially with the constant accessibility provided by technology, but you have to do it anyway. Create physical boundaries, such as turning off work-related notifications or having a designated workspace separate from your relaxation area.
- **Fear of Missing Out (FOMO):** This can discourage individuals from disconnecting. You need to constantly remind yourself it's okay to be behind some things.
- **Guilt and perceived expectations:** To overcome this barrier, remind yourself that breaks are necessary for your well-being and productivity. Remember, taking care of yourself allows you to perform better in the long run.
- **Habits and mindset:** Prioritize breaks. Rearrange your schedule to include breaks into your daily routine and reinforce the habit by scheduling them and treating them as non-negotiable.
- **Lack of awareness:** Sometimes, individuals may not fully realize the negative consequences of not taking breaks or disconnecting. The solution: Educate yourself about the importance of breaks for well-being and productivity.
- **Workload and deadlines:** Heavy workloads and impending deadlines can make it challenging to take breaks. Prioritize and plan your tasks effectively,

ensuring that breaks are factored into your schedule without compromising productivity.

TAKING BREAKS TO PREVENT DECISION FATIGUE

Decision-making is a complex mental process that requires focus, analysis, and sound judgment. However, as the day progresses and we take part in a series of decisions, our cognitive abilities can become fatigued, resulting in a phenomenon called *decision fatigue*.

Here's why breaks are powerful:

- **Gaining perspective:** By taking a break, you create distance from the immediate situation, enabling you to view the problem from a new angle. This renewed perspective can lead to more creative and effective solutions.
- **Improved decision accuracy:** When fatigued, decision-makers tend to make errors and overlook critical details. This new-found focus reduces the likelihood of errors, improves decision accuracy, and prevents costly mistakes.
- **Nurturing creativity:** Breaks stimulate creativity by providing mental space for new ideas and connections to form. Engaging in unrelated activities during a break activates different parts of the brain.
- **Reducing impulsive decisions:** Decision fatigue often leads to short-term thinking and an inability to consider long-term implications. Breaks provide an

opportunity to step back and reflect on the bigger picture.

- **Restoring mental energy:** Continuous decision-making drains mental resources. Breaks give your mind the opportunity to calm down. When you return to the decision-making process after a break, you are better equipped to make well-considered choices.

THE ART OF PURSUING CREATIVE BREAKS

While breaks provide an opportunity to recharge and relax, they can also be a valuable time to nurture your creativity. So take up creative activities during these breaks. They can offer a refreshing escape from work-related tasks and provide a platform for self-expression and exploration.

Here are ways to go about this:

- **Build a supportive and welcoming environment:** Set up a designated space where you can pursue your creative activities comfortably. Arrange your art supplies, musical instruments, or writing tools in an organized manner, making them easily accessible during your creative breaks.
- **Embrace mistakes and imperfections:** Don't be afraid to make mistakes or create imperfect pieces. Allow yourself the freedom to experiment, as it can lead to unexpected breakthroughs and innovative ideas.
- **Explore different techniques and styles:** Experiment with different techniques, styles, and mediums within

your chosen creative pursuit. For example, if you enjoy painting, try using different brush strokes, colors, or textures.

- **Identify your creative outlet:** Identify the creative activity that resonates with you the most. It could be writing, painting, playing a musical instrument, photography, crafting, or any other form of creative expression that sparks your interest.
- **Reflect and learn:** Notice what worked well and what didn't. Learn from your creative process and use these insights to refine your approach in future creative breaks.
- **Seek inspiration:** Visit art galleries, read books, listen to music, or explore nature. The idea is to find inspiration in the world around you and incorporate it into your creative breaks.
- **Share and collaborate:** Join art communities, writing groups, or music circles where you can receive feedback, exchange ideas, and gain inspiration from others.

WHAT YOU NEED TO KNOW ABOUT RESTORATIVE BREAKS

Restorative breaks go beyond simple relaxation. They provide a deeper level of rejuvenation. They help restore energy, focus, and total mental and physical health.

Here are things to know about restorative breaks:

- **Intentional reentry:** After a restorative break, have an intentional reentry process. It could be something simple (like reading work-related guidelines).
- **Duration and frequency:** This will depend on your schedule and personal preferences.
- **Purposeful rest:** Restorative breaks involve intentionally setting aside time for activities that aren't mere activities. The idea is to take a break for relaxation, restoration, and renewal.

DID YOU KNOW?

Did you know that the Pomodoro Technique can revolutionize your productivity and prevent burnout? Developed by Francesco Cirillo, this lesser-known time management method can work wonders.

Here's how it works: You set a timer for a focused work session, traditionally 25 minutes, known as a "Pomodoro." Once the timer goes off, you take a quick or short break, typically around 5 or 10 minutes. After completing four Pomodoros, you may now reward yourself and take a more extended break of 30 minutes.

It's a structured approach. Among its lineup of productivity-related benefits? It helps maintain focus, prevents mental fatigue, and enhances efficiency.

9

SEEKING PROFESSIONAL HELP

D id you go through all the steps mentioned in the *5-Step Burnout Resilience Formula* and find it's not working for you? That's fine—it's no big deal.

All you need to do is ask for help from a professional. Let them walk you through the ins and outs of the recovery process for burnout.

In this chapter, we'll talk about the need to seek professional help. We'll discuss the benefits of professional help, the types of professionals who can help you, different therapy options, and more.

This way, you'll have everything you need to know about the process. And because of the knowledge you got, you can feel more comfortable about seeing a professional about your issue with burnout.

THE NEED TO DESTIGMATIZE MENTAL HEALTH CARE (AND PROMOTE HELP-SEEKING BEHAVIOR)

Inarguably, mental health is important, yet burnout stigma and misunderstanding have long surrounded it. Some people think it's not important and definitely unnecessary. In a report featured in the *United Nations'* blog, the pandemic significantly affected how mental health care providers offered their services —so much so that the majority of providers stopped offering critical mental health care services (Alaoui, 2021).

Here's why:

- **Advocates for equality and human rights:** By destigmatizing mental health care, we promote equality and social justice. Everyone deserves access to high-quality mental health care, regardless of their condition or background.
- **Encourages help-seeking behavior:** Stigma creates a culture of silence and shame. It makes individuals reluctant to seek help for their mental health concerns.
- **Enhances treatment compliance:** When individuals face stigma, they may feel embarrassed or ashamed about their condition. Destigmatizing mental health care can help individuals feel more comfortable discussing their concerns.
- **Supports productivity and overall wellness:** Mental health issues can dramatically affect an individual's productivity, both at work and in their personal life. Destigmatization can resolve this and create supportive

environments that promote well-being and productivity.

BENEFITS OF PROFESSIONAL HELP

Mental health professionals offer specialized expertise and support in navigating burnout, providing valuable insights and coping strategies.

Here's a look at what professional help can do:

- **Accountability and progress monitoring:** Regular sessions provide structure, accountability, and opportunities to track progress and make necessary adjustments.
- **Coping strategies and stress management techniques:** Professionals equip you with effective tools to manage stress, improve self-care, and enhance resilience.
- **A holistic approach to healing:** Professionals consider various aspects of your life, helping you understand and address the underlying causes of burnout.
- **Objective assessment and diagnosis:** Professionals can accurately diagnose burnout and differentiate it from other conditions, ensuring targeted and effective treatment.
- **Personalized treatment plans:** Through personalized approaches, professionals develop strategies to address unique needs. As a result, this enhances the likelihood of successful outcomes.

- **Validation and emotional support:** Asking for professional help provides a safe and nonjudgmental space to express emotions, gain perspective, and receive empathetic support.

TYPES OF PROFESSIONALS WHO CAN HELP

Many professionals can provide expertise and support to help individuals address and overcome burnout. With how debilitating burnout can be, it's advisable to approach a professional who can assist you in the best way possible.

Here are people who can help:

- **Alternative practitioners:** Alternative practitioners such as acupuncturists, yoga instructors, or massage therapists may offer complementary approaches to managing stress, inducing a sense of relaxation, and supporting overall well-being in individuals experiencing burnout.
- **Coaches or mentors:** Burnout coaches or mentors can provide guidance, accountability, and support in navigating work-related challenges, setting goals, and making positive changes in your professional life.
- **Mindfulness instructors:** Mindfulness instructors specialize in teaching techniques that introduce present-moment awareness and stress reduction, which can be beneficial for managing burnout.
- **Nutritionists or dietitians:** These professionals can offer guidance on nutrition and diet, which can play a

role in managing burnout and supporting overall well-being.

- **Occupational therapists:** Occupational therapists can help individuals experiencing burnout by assessing their work environment and providing strategies for managing workload.
- **Psychiatrists or psychologists:** These professionals are trained to diagnose and treat mental health conditions, including burnout. They can provide therapy and prescribe medication if needed.
- **Sleep specialists:** Sleep specialists can address sleep-related issues that often accompany burnout and provide strategies for improving sleep quality and duration.
- **Therapists or counselors:** These mental health professionals specialize in talk therapy and can assist you in exploring and addressing the underlying causes of burnout, developing coping strategies, and improving emotional well-being.

THE PROCESS OF SEEKING PROFESSIONAL HELP

The process of seeking professional help for burnout involves key steps. After all, seeking professional help is a proactive step toward self-care and wellness, and the process may differ from individual to individual based on preferences and circumstances.

Here are the steps:

- **Active participation and commitment:** Be part of the treatment process and follow the professional's recommendations. This may involve attending regular sessions, practicing self-care strategies, implementing lifestyle changes, and actively participating in therapy or coaching exercises.
- **Building a therapeutic relationship:** Establishing a trusting and supportive therapeutic relationship is important. It allows you to openly communicate and feel understood.
- **Identifying the need for help:** The first step is acknowledging and accepting that burnout is affecting your wellness and that seeking professional help is necessary.
- **Progress evaluation and adjustments:** Evaluate the effectiveness of the treatment plan and adjust (as necessary) to address new needs or challenges.
- **Researching and selecting a professional:** Conduct thorough research to identify professionals who specialize in burnout or related areas. Consider factors like their experience, qualifications, and therapeutic approaches.
- **Scheduling an initial consultation or appointment:** Contact the chosen professional. Then, discuss your concerns, learn more about their approach, and determine if you feel comfortable working with them.
- **Sharing your concerns and experiences:** Openly share your experiences, symptoms, and any challenges you're

facing due to burnout. Be honest and provide relevant details to help the professional understand your situation better.

ADDITIONAL WAYS TO SEEK PROFESSIONAL HELP

Sometimes, finding professional help won't be easy, even if you've followed the process above. It takes time and patience. The solution is to consider other options.

Here's what you can do:

- **Ask for a free phone consultation:** Many professionals offer free phone consultations to discuss your concerns. Use this opportunity to ask questions about their approach, treatment plans, and any specific strategies they use for addressing burnout.
- **Check with your insurance provider:** If you have health insurance, contact your provider to understand what mental health services are covered and what providers are in-network.
- **Consider specialized expertise:** Depending on your specific burnout-related needs, you may benefit from professionals who specialize in certain areas. For example, some professionals may have expertise in workplace stress, career transitions, or holistic approaches to burnout recovery.
- **Consider teletherapy options:** Teletherapy or counseling services are offered remotely. They

eliminate the need to commute and waiting room delays.

- **Consider the importance of cultural competence:** If cultural background or identity is important to you, seek professionals who have experience working with individuals from diverse backgrounds.
- **Consult with your primary care physician:** Your primary care physician is a valuable resource. They may have referrals to trusted professionals or be able to provide guidance based on their knowledge of your medical history.
- **Trust your personal preferences:** Each person has unique preferences when it comes to seeking professional help. Some may prefer a therapist of a specific gender, while others may prioritize someone who shares their cultural background or speaks their native language.
- **Use online directories and resources:** Online directories and platforms dedicated to mental health can be helpful. These platforms often provide detailed profiles, treatment approaches, and contact information.

HOW TO DEAL WITH THE COST OF PROFESSIONAL HELP

Getting professional help isn't free. Considering the accessibility and cost of professional help is important when seeking support for your mental health or dealing with burnout.

Here's how you can proceed:

- **Assess your financial situation:** Take a close look at your financial resources and consider what you can afford in terms of professional help. Evaluate your budget and determine how much you are willing and able to allocate towards therapy or counseling services.
- **Check insurance coverage:** Review your policy to understand the extent of mental health coverage it provides. Look for information on in-network providers, copayments, deductibles, and any limitations or restrictions that may apply.
- **Consider community mental health centers:** Community mental health centers are often funded by government agencies or local organizations and offer a range of mental health services at reduced fees or on a sliding scale.
- **Consider proximity and transportation:** Evaluate the practicality of traveling to appointments and consider the associated costs, such as transportation expenses or parking fees.
- **Inquire about payment options:** Some professionals may offer flexible payment options based on your income or financial circumstances. Ask if they have any discounted rates or payment plans available.
- **Look for community resources:** These organizations often have sliding-scale fees or subsidized programs to make professional help more accessible to those in need. Reach out to local clinics, universities, or mental health centers to inquire about these options.

- **Seek out pro bono services:** Look for organizations or therapists in your area who participate in pro bono programs or offer reduced fees. These services can provide valuable support while minimizing the financial burden.

TRACKING PROGRESS, VISUALIZING SUCCESS, AND MAKING ADJUSTMENTS

According to a research paper that explores the subject of adaptability, it's an excellent idea to always keep tabs on how you're doing (Singh et al., 2021). By actively monitoring progress, tracking success, and making adjustments along the way, individuals can optimize their therapy experience. They can also increase the likelihood of achieving meaningful and sustainable outcomes in overcoming burnout.

Here's what needs to be done:

- **Adjusting treatment approaches:** Based on ongoing monitoring and feedback, therapists may modify the treatment approach as needed. This could involve refining techniques, introducing new interventions, or exploring different therapeutic modalities.
- **Continuing self-care and support:** Emphasize the importance of self-care practices outside of therapy sessions. These efforts complement the therapy process and contribute to overall well-being and burnout prevention.

- **Establishing baseline measures:** At the beginning of the therapy or intervention, it's important to objectively assess the severity of burnout symptoms and overall well-being. This may involve self-report assessments, behavioral observations, or standardized scales to track progress over time.
- **Feedback and communication with the therapist:** Maintain open and honest communication with the therapist about your progress, concerns, and any challenges faced.
- **Goal setting and outcome measurement:** Collaboratively set specific and measurable goals with your therapist to target areas of improvement and desired outcomes.
- **Monitoring and relapse prevention for the long haul:** Even after significant progress, continue monitoring your well-being and remain vigilant for any signs of relapse.
- **Regular therapy sessions:** Regular sessions provide opportunities to collaborate with the therapist on adapting strategies to address emerging issues.
- **Self-reflection and journaling:** Self-reflect and journal to record personal insights, challenges, and progress made throughout the treatment process. This can identify patterns and provide information for therapy discussions.
- **Tracking symptom changes:** Monitor changes in burnout symptoms, such as exhaustion, cynicism, and reduced professional efficacy. Periodic assessments can

provide insights into the effectiveness of therapeutic interventions.

EXPLORING THERAPY OPTIONS: FINDING THE RIGHT FIT

A perk of working with a professional? You can collaborate on a treatment plan. This may include therapy sessions, goal setting, stress management techniques, lifestyle adjustments, and other interventions aimed at addressing your specific needs and facilitating recovery from burnout.

Here are the options:

- **Cognitive-behavioral therapy (CBT):** Examine the benefits of CBT, a widely used therapy approach that focuses on identifying and changing negative thought patterns and behaviors contributing to burnout.
- **Group therapy:** Investigate the potential benefits of group therapy, where individuals experiencing burnout come together to share experiences, support one another, and learn from each other's perspectives.
- **Integrative or eclectic therapy:** Consider the advantages of integrative or eclectic therapy approaches that combine elements from various therapeutic modalities.
- **Mindfulness-based therapy:** Explore the principles of mindfulness-based therapies, such as mindfulness-based stress reduction (MBSR) or mindfulness-based cognitive therapy (MBCT).

- **Online therapy:** Explore the convenience and accessibility of online therapy platforms. They offer the opportunity to connect with therapists virtually.
- **Other complementary approaches:** Consider complementary therapies that may support individuals in managing burnout. Exploring these modalities can provide alternative avenues for self-expression and stress reduction.
- **Psychodynamic therapy:** Investigate the insights and benefits of unconscious patterns and past experiences. Plus, discuss how this therapy approach can facilitate insight, emotional healing, and personal growth.
- **Solution-focused therapy:** Look at the key principles of solution-focused therapy: they emphasize the need for identifying and building on individual strengths, resources, and solutions.

CHALLENGING STEREOTYPES AND MISCONCEPTIONS SURROUNDING MENTAL HEALTH

Despite its integral part, mental health is often plagued by stereotypes and misconceptions that perpetuate stigma and hinder progress. Challenging these deep-seated beliefs and shifting perspectives is how we can nurture understanding, empathy, and support for individuals facing mental health challenges.

Here's more about the subject:

- **Amplifying diverse voices:** By sharing their stories and perspectives, we can challenge stereotypes and provide a more nuanced understanding of mental health.
- **Dismantling the "weakness" myth:** A prevailing stereotype surrounding mental health is the belief that individuals with mental health conditions are weak or lacking in willpower. This misconception undermines the immense strength and resilience individuals with mental health challenges demonstrate in navigating their struggles.
- **Encouraging mental health education:** By incorporating mental health education into schools, workplaces, and communities, we can raise awareness and understanding of mental health conditions.
- **Integrating mental health into public discourse:** Shifting perspectives requires integrating mental health into public discourse and making it a priority in policy discussions.
- **Promoting a holistic view of recovery:** Recovery is a personal journey, and it differs for each individual. It may involve managing symptoms, developing coping strategies, and living a meaningful life despite ongoing challenges.
- **Recognizing the complexity of mental health:** By recognizing the complexity of mental health, we can move away from oversimplified narratives and understand each individual's unique experience.

- **Separating mental health from violence:** In reality, the majority of individuals with mental health conditions are not violent; they are more likely to be victims of violence themselves.

THE SUBJECT OF BARRIERS TO SEEKING SUPPORT FOR MENTAL HEALTH

Access to mental health support is valuable for individuals experiencing mental health challenges. However, many barriers often prevent people from seeking and receiving the care they need. To ensure that mental health support is accessible to all, we need to bridge the gap and break down these barriers.

Here's what you need to know:

- **Addressing financial barriers:** Financial limitations can stand in the way. High costs of therapy, medication, and other treatment options can be prohibitive.
- **Culturally competent and inclusive care:** Cultural and linguistic barriers can create significant challenges in accessing mental health support. It's best to provide culturally competent care that respects and addresses the diverse needs of individuals from different backgrounds.
- **Increasing accessibility of services:** It's recommended to increase the availability of mental health resources in both urban and rural areas. This may involve expanding mental health programs, recruiting and training more

mental health professionals, and providing telehealth options.

- **Integrating mental health into primary care:** Many individuals initially seek help for mental health concerns through primary care providers. This approach is more holistic.
- **Providing supportive environments:** Creating supportive environments in schools, workplaces, and communities is best. With supportive environments, those who need mental health care can feel comfortable when asking for it.
- **Targeted outreach and public awareness campaigns:** Engaging in targeted outreach and public awareness campaigns can reach individuals who may be unaware of available mental health resources or hesitant to seek help.

MEASURING THE EFFECTIVENESS OF BURNOUT PREVENTION PROGRAMS

Measuring the effectiveness of burnout prevention programs is necessary for organizations. It's how they can understand the impact of their initiatives and make important decisions regarding employee wellness.

Here are things to consider:

- **Analyze program participation and engagement:** Monitor attendance rates, completion rates of program components, and feedback from participants. Higher engagement and active involvement often indicate a higher likelihood of program effectiveness.
- **Collect qualitative feedback:** In addition to quantitative data, gather qualitative feedback through interviews, focus groups, or open-ended survey questions.
- **Compare data to benchmarks or control groups:** To gain a better understanding of the program's impact, consider comparing the data to industry benchmarks or control groups.
- **Conduct pre- and post-program assessments:** Collect data before the intervention and after its implementation. This data provides a groundwork for comparison.
- **Continuous improvement:** Use the evaluation results to ensure continuous improvement of the burnout prevention program. Identify areas that need adjustment and make necessary modifications.
- **Long-term follow-up:** Monitor the long-term effects by conducting follow-up assessments at regular intervals. This allows for understanding whether the program's effects are sustainable over time.
- **Monitor changes in organizational indicators:** Look beyond individual-level measures and observe changes in broader organizational indicators. Positive changes

in these indicators can suggest the effectiveness of the burnout prevention program at the organizational level.

- **Test burnout levels:** Use standardized assessment tools such as the Maslach Burnout Inventory (MBI) or the Oldenburg Burnout Inventory (OLBI) to measure burnout levels before and after the program.
- **Test stress levels:** Assess employees' perceived stress levels using validated scales such as the Perceived Stress Scale (PSS). This metric can help determine whether the program has effectively reduced perceived stress among participants.

WHAT IF YOU FALL OFF THE WAGON?

If you tried treating burnout before and failed, that's okay. Accept the fact that sometimes things may not work out as well as you anticipated. You can be sad or feel miserable about it temporarily. However, at some point, you need to get back out there and try again.

Here's a discussion that can help:

- **Acceptance and self-compassion:** Recognize that setbacks and relapses are a normal part of the recovery process. Practice self-compassion by acknowledging that everyone faces challenges and slips along the way.
- **Learn from it:** Consider it a remarkable experience and think of it as an opportunity to expand your knowledge. Consider what lessons can be gained from

the experience and how it can inform your approach moving forward.

- **Modify your approach:** Assess whether any adjustments need to be made to your treatment plan or strategies. Collaborate with your therapist or counselor to explore new approaches, techniques, or interventions.
- **Reflect on triggers and patterns:** Identify triggers and patterns. These things can help you develop strategies to address them effectively in the future.
- **Revisit coping strategies:** Revisit the coping strategies and techniques that have previously worked for you. This may include stress-management techniques, self-care practices, or specific tools provided by your therapist.
- **Stay committed and persistent:** Stay persistent in your efforts, even when facing setbacks. Remember that the way forward isn't always obstacle-free.

DID YOU KNOW?

Did you know that intentionally creating a clean, organized, and inspiring physical environment in the workplace has a deep impact on well-being and mindset?

This practice is referred to as resetting the room. It involves decluttering workspaces, organizing materials, and incorporating elements like plants or artwork. This practice eliminates visual distractions and fosters a sense of calm and focus. It also provides an opportunity for brief breaks and mindfulness exercises.

By consciously resetting the room, individuals create a harmonious workspace that supports well-being and prevents burnout. Taking just a few minutes to reset the room can make a significant difference in productivity and overall work experience.

10

LIFE AFTER BURNOUT RECOVERY

E ven after recovering from burnout, you can get caught up in it again. This is why I always try to start my day with easy-to-do and quick activities (like making my bed or putting my clothes away). This is also my approach to work-related activities.

When I start my work, I always look for a couple of projects I can finish quickly (like an email or paying a bill). They are more than just tasks I can do easily and quickly (in less than five minutes); they're things that give me a sense of accomplishment. They remind me to take things slowly and attend to the other tasks waiting for me—one task at a time.

Following just one or two of the steps from the *5-Step Burnout Resilience Formula* may result in wasted efforts (or you'll recover yet be burned out again in the next few days). If you follow everything, though, you'll realize you'll be burnout-free one of these days.

You also have to keep going. The formula may be powerful, but it's no magic pill. It works wonders—there's no question about that. But remember, it only works wonders for you if you do the work. If you don't commit to the five steps, you can't expect the formula to work.

In this final chapter, that's what we'll get into. We'll talk about everything you need to know about life after recovering from burnout.

REDISCOVERING YOUR PURPOSE

In the middle of life's constant demands and distractions, taking the time to rediscover our personal identity and purpose is vital. Through introspection and self-reflection, we can explore our values, passions, and strengths and align them with our intrinsic motivations. Investing our time in activities we love, connecting with like-minded individuals, and practicing mindfulness and self-care all contribute to this process.

Here's what you can do:

- **Connect with like-minded individuals:** Seek out communities, groups, or organizations that share your values and interests. Surrounding yourself with supportive and inspiring people can provide a sense of belonging and help clarify your beliefs and aspirations.
- **Embrace the ongoing journey:** Recognize that personal identity and purpose can evolve over time. Embrace curiosity and openness to explore new possibilities and redefine your sense of self as needed.

- **Explore different perspectives:** Step outside of your comfort zone and actively seek out diverse perspectives and experiences. This broadens your understanding of the world and can lead to new insights about yourself and your purpose.
- **Pursue joyful activities:** Engage in hobbies, creative projects, or activities that bring you joy and fulfillment. Exploring new experiences can uncover hidden talents and further define your sense of self.
- **Revisit childhood interests:** Reflect on the activities and interests that sparked joy and curiosity during your childhood. Revisiting these passions can reignite a sense of purpose and remind you of your authentic self.
- **Seek solitude:** Find moments of solitude and silence to disconnect from external influences and distractions. This allows for deeper introspection and self-discovery.
- **Welcome vulnerability:** Allow yourself to be vulnerable and open to exploring deeper layers of your identity. Embracing vulnerability can lead to self-discovery, personal growth, and a greater sense of purpose.

ANTI-BURNOUT TRENDS IN THE MODERN WORKPLACE

Employers understand the detrimental effects that can arise for employees, which is why they proactively implement various programs. Additionally, they provide resources like employee assistance programs and designated wellness rooms to support their workforce's overall wellness and take a stand against burnout.

Here are popular trends:

- **Bare Minimum Mondays:** Some organizations focus on essential tasks and prioritize self-care. This trend aims to combat burnout by reducing overwhelming workloads and promoting a balanced approach to productivity.
- **Employee well-being surveys:** Their goal is to gauge the overall satisfaction and stress levels within the organization, allowing for targeted interventions and initiatives to prevent burnout and support employee well-being.
- **Mental health days:** Some companies implement policies that specifically allow employees to take mental health days off. This trend acknowledges the need for mental and emotional wellness.
- **Mindful email practices:** They're all about teaching mindful email practices, such as setting clear boundaries for after-work hours, encouraging concise and respectful communication, and reducing email and overload.
- **Peer recognition programs:** They set peer recognition programs where employees can acknowledge and appreciate each other's contributions. As a result, they end up fostering a positive and supportive work culture.

- **Peer support networks:** Organizations are encouraging the formation of peer support networks. These networks foster a sense of belonging, encourage open communication, and create a supportive community within the workplace.
- **Sabbaticals and extended time off:** These trends allow employees to take a significant break from work to recharge, pursue personal interests, or engage in self-reflection.
- **Transparent communication:** They're about encouraging transparent and open communication across all levels of the organization, ensuring employees feel heard, valued, and well-informed.
- **Wellness challenges:** Employers implement wellness challenges or programs that promote healthy habits, such as physical activity, healthy eating, and stress reduction techniques.
- **Wellness rooms:** Many workplaces are creating designated wellness rooms or relaxation spaces where employees can take breaks, engage in mindfulness activities, or simply recharge.
- **Workplace wellness apps:** These apps offer features like guided meditation, fitness challenges, sleep tracking, and stress management tools.

SELF-CARE RITUALS AND DAILY PRACTICES

Creating daily self-care rituals lets us nurture and recharge ourselves. We actively prioritize our well-being by incorporating intentional practices into our routines. Each morning, we begin with activities like stretching, meditation, or journaling, setting a calm and centered tone for the day. Then, do what you can to ensure you spend the rest of the day with a happy mind and heart.

Here are examples of self-care rituals you'd like to try:

- **Aromatherapy ritual:** Use essential oils or scented candles to create a soothing ambiance and enhance relaxation during self-care activities.
- **Daily affirmations:** Recite positive affirmations or mantras to uplift and encourage yourself, fostering self-confidence and a positive mindset.
- **Digital sunset ritual:** Establish a specific time each evening to disconnect from electronic devices and engage in screen-free activities.
- **Evening self-care routine:** Engage in a calming evening routine that includes activities like a warm bath, a skincare ritual, and reading a book before bed to facilitate relaxation and better sleep.
- **Reading ritual:** Carve out time each day to read books that inspire, educate, or entertain you, allowing for escapism and expanding your knowledge.
- **Self-care spa night:** Create a spa-like atmosphere at home with soothing music, a warm bath, facial masks,

and body treatments to pamper and rejuvenate your body and mind.

EMPLOYEE ASSISTANCE PROGRAMS BY EMPLOYERS

Employee Assistance Programs (EAPs) play a big role in minimizing both absenteeism and presenteeism. By addressing the root causes and offering assistance, EAPs enable employees to effectively manage their overall wellness and lessen the negative effects of personal challenges on their job performance.

Here are examples of the EAPs they offer:

- **Counseling services:** EAPs often provide access to confidential counseling services where employees can receive professional support for personal or work-related issues such as stress, anxiety, relationship problems, or grief.
- **Crisis intervention:** These programs can offer immediate crisis intervention services for employees facing emergencies or traumatic events, providing access to 24/7 helplines or counseling services.
- **Financial counseling:** They're all about financial counseling services to assist employees in managing their finances, budgeting, debt management, or financial planning.
- **Health and wellness programs:** Some EAPs include wellness programs that promote physical and mental wellness (like fitness challenges, smoking cessation programs, and stress management workshops).

- **Legal assistance:** Some EAPs include legal consultation services where employees can receive guidance on legal matters such as estate planning, family law, or consumer rights.
- **Managerial consultation:** Such programs may offer support for managers or supervisors. The goal is to help them address employee issues, handle conflicts, or improve communication within their teams.
- **Mental health resources:** EAPs may offer resources and information on mental health topics, including educational materials, self-help resources, and referrals to mental health professionals.
- **Referral services:** EAPs can connect employees with community resources, support groups, or specialized professionals based on their specific needs.
- **Work-life balance support:** EAPs may provide resources and assistance to help employees balance their work and personal lives. It includes parenting support, elder care guidance, or referrals to childcare services.

LEVERAGING ASMR

Autonomous Sensory Meridian Response (ASMR) comes with an infallible ability to induce relaxation and sensory stimulation. Because of this, you can use it to create a more soothing and stress-free environment in the workplace.

Here are ways you can use ASMR:

- **ASMR playlists:** Share curated ASMR playlists or provide other employees with resources to explore ASMR content during their breaks or while working remotely.
- **ASMR stations:** Set up designated areas in break rooms or common areas with ASMR triggers, like sensory boards with different textures. These stations allow employees to engage in calming activities during their breaks, helping them recharge and reduce stress levels.
- **Guided relaxation sessions:** Conduct short guided relaxation sessions during break times where employees can listen to a recorded ASMR session or a mindfulness exercise.
- **Noise-canceling headphones:** Give everyone noise-canceling headphones to help create a quieter work environment, reduce distractions, and promote focus.
- **Quiet spaces:** Designate areas where everyone can relax and rejuvenate for a few minutes. These spaces can be equipped with comfortable seating, soft lighting, and ASMR-triggering items like sound machines or gentle nature sounds to create a serene atmosphere.
- **Soft background sounds:** Play soft background music or ambient ASMR sounds, such as raindrops or gentle ocean waves.
- **Virtual backgrounds:** Offer ASMR-inspired virtual backgrounds during video conferences or remote meetings. It can create a visually soothing environment. Examples include serene nature scenes, gentle

movement patterns, or animated visuals designed to induce relaxation.

- **Whispering techniques:** Encourage speakers to use soft-spoken voices or whispering techniques during presentations or discussions. It can create a more relaxed and attentive atmosphere.

THE ART OF CONTINUOUS LEARNING

Continuous learning involves actively seeking personal development opportunities and expanding knowledge and skills. It requires engaging in formal education, attending seminars, and participating in workshops to acquire new expertise and stay up to date with advancements.

It's also about self-directed exploration through reading, listening to educational content, and using online learning platforms. By adopting a mindset of continuous learning, individuals take charge of their own development, remain adaptable, and continually strive to enhance their understanding and abilities, enabling them to thrive in an ever-evolving world.

Here's what you can do:

- **Connect with a learning community:** Engage with like-minded individuals. Join forums, attend meetups, or participate in online communities to build and develop meaningful connections and gain support and inspiration.
- **Dive into microlearning:** Break down your learning. Instead of overwhelming yourself with long study

sessions, engage in short bursts of focused learning throughout the day.

- **Embrace the different means of learning:** Explore diverse subjects and learning methods to keep your learning journey interesting and engaging. Mix up reading, online courses, workshops, and interactive experiences to maintain enthusiasm.
- **Get feedback and reflection:** Reach out to mentors, respectable peers, or educators to gain insights into your learning progress. Reflect on your learning experiences, identify areas for improvement, and make adjustments accordingly.
- **Leverage active learning:** Instead of passively consuming information, actively engage with the material. Take notes, ask questions, and apply what you've learned through practice and real-life scenarios.
- **Reflect on your progress:** Reflect on what you have learned and how it has impacted your personal and professional growth. Celebrate your achievements and use feedback to guide your future learning endeavors.

USING LAUGHTER THERAPY

Laughter therapy, also known as humor therapy, is an ever-powerful tool for boosting mood and reducing stress. It involves finding the power of humor and embracing moments of lightheartedness to bring joy and relaxation to our lives.

By consciously incorporating laughter into our lives, we tap into its transformative power. As a result, we navigate challenges with a lighter perspective, cultivate resilience, and improve emotional and mental wellness.

Here are some ways to use laughter therapy:

- **Be playful:** Embrace your inner child and engage in playful activities, such as playing games, engaging in imaginative play, or engaging in activities that bring out your sense of humor.
- **Read funny books or comics:** Explore humorous books, comics, or satirical literature that can transport you to a world of laughter and amusement.
- **Share jokes and funny stories:** Exchange jokes and funny anecdotes with friends, family, or colleagues, creating moments of shared laughter and lightheartedness.
- **Sign up for laughter yoga:** Join a laughter yoga class or practice laughter exercises on your own. Laughter yoga combines deep breathing techniques and laughter exercises to promote well-being and stress reduction.
- **Spend time with funny friends:** Seek the company of friends or loved ones who have a great sense of humor and can make you laugh. Share funny stories, engage in playful banter, or plan activities that bring joy and laughter.
- **Surround yourself with humor:** Decorate your living or working space with humorous quotes, cartoons, or funny pictures that can elicit spontaneous laughter and lift your spirits.

- **Use self-deprecating humor:** Light-heartedly laugh at yourself and find humor in your quirks and imperfections. This can help you maintain a humble and lighthearted perspective.
- **Watch comedy shows or movies:** Tune in to comedy shows, sitcoms, or humorous movies that tickle your funny bone and bring a smile to your face.
- **Watch stand-up comedy:** Attend stand-up comedy shows or watch recorded performances of comedians who resonate with your sense of humor.

THE ADVANTAGE OF A SOLO RETREAT

Solo retreats provide a remarkable opportunity to take dedicated time for yourself in a peaceful environment, enabling reflection, rejuvenation, and reconnection with your inner self. By temporarily disconnecting from the demands of daily life and immersing yourself in solitude, you can gain clarity, recharge your energy, and foster personal growth.

During a solo retreat, you can engage in activities such as journaling, meditation, hiking in nature, practicing yoga, reading, or simply enjoying moments of silence. This intentional time away from distractions allows for self-reflection, deep introspection, and the cultivation of a deeper understanding of oneself.

How to take solo retreats:

- **Dive into personal development books:** Select personal development books that resonate with you and explore them during your solo retreat. Engage in deep reading sessions and take notes to internalize the wisdom and apply it to your own personal growth journey.
- **Embrace silence and solitude:** Allow yourself moments of quiet contemplation, solitude, and stillness, enabling deep introspection and the cultivation of inner peace.
- **Engage in introspective activities:** Reflect on your goals, values, and aspirations through journaling, deep contemplation, and setting intentions for personal growth.
- **Find a serene location:** Choose a tranquil setting, such as a cabin in the woods, a beachside cottage, or a quiet retreat center, where you can immerse yourself in solitude.
- **Make a vision board or mind map:** Engage in visual expression by creating a vision board or mind map that represents your aspirations, dreams, and goals. Use images, words, and symbols to visually manifest your intentions and inspire yourself during and after the retreat.
- **Read inspirational books:** Choose books that inspire and nourish your mind, exploring topics such as personal growth, spirituality, or philosophy to expand your perspective.

THE POWER OF RANDOM ACTS OF KINDNESS

Random acts of kindness are powerful gestures that have the ability to spread positivity and compassion throughout our communities. By engaging in small acts of kindness towards others, we create a ripple effect of goodwill, fostering a sense of connection and purpose.

Here are some things you can do:

- **Leave a positive and uplifting note for someone to find:** Leave an anonymous note with kind words in a public place or for a friend, brightening their day and reminding them of the goodness in the world.
- **Offer to babysit for a friend or family member:** Provide a much-needed break for a parent by offering to watch their children, giving them an opportunity to relax or take care of personal errands.
- **Offer to help an elderly neighbor with their groceries or household tasks:** Extend a helping hand to an elderly neighbor by assisting them with their groceries or offering help with household chores, showing kindness and support to those who may need it.
- **Offer to walk a neighbor's dog or pet sit while they are away:** Assist a neighbor by offering to take care of their pets, ensuring their furry friends are well-cared for, and alleviating any worries while they are away.
- **Pay for the coffee or meal of the person behind you in line:** Surprise someone by paying for their order,

spreading a moment of joy, and creating a chain of generosity.

- **Plant a tree or flowers in a public space:** Help beautify your community by planting trees or flowers in a park or public area, creating a welcoming and refreshing environment for all to enjoy.

- **Send a heartfelt thank-you note to someone who has made a difference in your life:** Express your gratitude through a thoughtful note to someone who has positively impacted your life.

- **Support a local business:** Choose to shop at a local business or leave a positive review online, supporting the growth and success of small businesses in your community.

- **Volunteer at a local charity or community organization:** Dedicate your time and skills to a charitable cause or community organization, contributing to the betterment of your community and making a positive impact on the lives of others.

- **Write a heartfelt letter or send a care package to a deployed service member:** Show appreciation and support for those serving in the military by sending a thoughtful letter or care package, brightening their day and reminding them of the love and gratitude from home.

DID YOU KNOW?

Did you know that there are employers who want their employees to strike a balance between their work and life?

Because these employers believe employees are only at their sharpest when they aren't burned out, they allow them to have You Only Live Once (YOLO) days where they can engage in practices that border on relaxation and memorable experiences.

To cite a specific case, there's Conductor, a cloud-based marketing platform. The higher-ups of the company gave employees a month for such practices. The company went big on giving people the liberty to maximize time (Ali, 2022).

YOU CAN HELP SOMEONE ELSE TO BREAK THE CYCLE

As you gain back control and begin to break the burnout cycle, it's natural that you'll want to help others do the same – and you can do that right now.

Simply by sharing your honest opinion of this book and a little about your own story, you'll show new readers where they can find the guidance they're looking for to help them overcome work stress.

WANT TO HELP OTHERS?

Thank you for your support... It makes more difference than you realize.

CONCLUSION

Breaking the Burnout Cycle at Work: A Comprehensive Guide to Conquer Job Exhaustion, Identify Sustainable Success, and Revitalize Your Career is not your run-of-the-mill book that covers the topic of burnout. Unlike the other books on the market, it tackles the need to address work burnout using five steps.

Here, we explored the debilitating effects of burnout in the workplace and the importance of understanding, preventing, and overcoming it. Throughout this journey, we explored the depths of job exhaustion, identified strategies for achieving sustainable success, and discovered ways to revitalize our careers.

The realities of modern work environments can often lead to a dangerous spiral of stress, fatigue, and disengagement. However, armed with knowledge and the right tools, we have the power to break free from this cycle and create a more fulfilling and balanced professional life.

As we conclude this guide, remember that staying on top of burnout is an ongoing process. It requires an unwavering commitment to personal growth, continuous self-reflection, and adaptation. By implementing the strategies and practices outlined in this book, we can proactively address burnout, reclaim our joy and passion for our work, and find renewed purpose in our careers.

WHY USE THE 5-STEP BURNOUT RESILIENCE FORMULA?

Each step in the *5-Step Burnout Resilience Formula* works because they address different aspects of our physical, mental, and emotional well-being. As they are, they contribute to a holistic approach to preventing and overcoming burnout.

Below, let's review each step.

Exercise

Regular exercise has many benefits for our overall well-being. It also helps to increase energy levels, enhance cognitive function, and improve sleep quality. By engaging in physical activity, we not only take care of our physical health but also reduce stress and boost our resilience to burnout.

Good Nutrition

A balanced and nutritious diet is important in supporting our physical and mental health. Proper nutrition provides our bodies with the necessary nutrients, vitamins, and minerals to function optimally. It helps regulate our energy levels, supports brain function, and enhances our immune system. When we nourish ourselves with healthy foods, we increase our resilience to stress, improve our overall well-being, and reduce the risk of burnout.

Quality Sleep

Sufficient and restorative sleep is what we need. It's essential for our bodies and minds to recover from daily stresses. When we're asleep, our bodies refuel, and our brains take in information and sort out memories. Lack of sleep can lead to fatigue, poor concentration, impaired decision-making, and increased vulnerability to stress. Prioritizing the need for adequate sleep allows us to recharge and replenish our energy.

Mindfulness and Meditation

Mindfulness and meditation practices cultivate present-moment awareness and help us develop a nonjudgmental and compassionate attitude toward ourselves and our experiences. These practices promote relaxation, reduce anxiety, and increase our ability to manage stress effectively. By incorporating mindfulness and meditation into our daily routine, we enhance our emotional well-being, improve focus and clarity, and develop resilience in the face of work-related pressures.

Take a Break from Work

Taking regular breaks from work is how you can achieve a work-life balance. So step away from your work, recharge, relax, and have fun. By disconnecting from work, we give ourselves the opportunity to nurture our relationships, pursue hobbies, and engage in self-care practices. These breaks help us replenish our energy, regain perspective, and prevent the accumulation of chronic stress that can lead to burnout.

A SUCCESS STORY

Let's go over the story of Arianna Huffington, a prominent figure in media and journalism who became widely recognized for her successful struggle with burnout. Her personal experience with burnout led her to reassess her priorities and make significant changes in her life, ultimately inspiring others to do the same.

As the co-founder of The Huffington Post, Arianna was known for her tireless work ethic and dedication. However, her relentless pursuit of success took a toll on her well-being, leading to exhaustion and burnout. It was a wake-up call that prompted her to reevaluate her approach to work and life.

Arianna's transformative journey began when she collapsed from exhaustion and sleep deprivation, hitting her head on a desk and sustaining an injury. This incident forced her to confront the consequences of her burnout and recognize the urgent need for change. Determined to prioritize her health and well-being, she made significant adjustments to her lifestyle and work habits.

She incorporated self-care practices into her routine, such as prioritizing sleep, practicing mindfulness and meditation, and embracing the importance of personal time. Additionally, she shifted her perspective on success, emphasizing the significance of well-being and fulfillment over conventional measures of achievement.

Arianna's journey toward overcoming burnout not only revitalized her own life but also inspired others to reassess their priorities and find a healthier balance. In *Thrive: The Third Metric to Redefining Success and Creating a Life of Well-Being, Wisdom, and Wonder*, she fills us in on her personal struggles and the indispensable life lessons she learned, encouraging individuals to prioritize self-care and well-being in their own lives (Huffington, 2014).

Her successful struggle with burnout serves as a testament to the transformative power of addressing and overcoming this pervasive issue. Arianna Huffington's story stands as a reminder that prioritizing self-care and well-being is not only crucial for personal happiness but also essential for sustained success and fulfillment in all areas of life.

FINAL THOUGHTS

Remember that every step you make—no matter how small—is a big step toward your goal. They're not much, but they're worth celebrating.

May this guide serve as a source of inspiration, empowerment, and guidance as you navigate your own journey toward breaking the vicious work burnout cycle. The goal is to embrace the knowledge you gained, take action, and unlock a future of sustainable success and fulfillment in your personal and professional life.

Finally, if you've enjoyed this book or would like to share a success story, please leave a review or a comment. I'd love to hear from you.

Good luck!

GLOSSARY

Absenteeism: The habitual or frequent absence of an individual from work or other obligations without a valid reason, which disrupts productivity and can be influenced by various factors.

Analytical thinker: It refers to an individual who employs a systematic and logical approach to problem-solving and decision-making. They actively gather and analyze information, identify patterns, and draw conclusions based on evidence.

ASMR (Autonomous Sensory Meridian Response): A pleasant, tingling sensation experienced in response to specific triggers, such as soft whispers or gentle sounds, often sought after for relaxation and stress relief.

Assertive leader: It refers to someone who confidently expresses their opinions, needs, and expectations while respecting the rights and perspectives of others. They actively communicate their vision and goals, delegate tasks effectively, and provide constructive feedback.

Bare Minimum Mondays: Refers to the practice of focusing on essential tasks or responsibilities on Mondays to start the week without overwhelming oneself.

Boundary management: The practice of establishing and maintaining healthy boundaries between work and personal life to prevent work burnout.

Burnout stigma: The negative perception and judgment surrounding burnout, which can discourage individuals from seeking help and support.

Baby boomers: The generation born between the mid-1940s and mid-1960s, known for their significant population increase following World War II.

Cogs in the machine: A metaphorical term used to describe individuals who feel like insignificant parts of a larger system, lacking autonomy or a sense of purpose in their work.

Diplomatic peacemaker: It refers to an individual who actively promotes harmony and resolves conflict through tactful communication, a strategic approach, and negotiation. They listen empathetically to different perspectives, seek common ground, and facilitate dialogue to find mutually beneficial solutions.

Digital overload: Overwhelming exposure to digital technologies and information, leading to cognitive fatigue and decreased productivity.

EAPs (Employee Assistance Programs): Employer-provided programs offering counseling, support services, and resources to help employees manage personal and work-related challenges, including burnout.

Emotional labor: It refers to the effort required to manage and regulate one's emotions in the workplace, including suppressing negative emotions, displaying desired emotions, and maintaining a professional demeanor, often leading to emotional exhaustion, increased stress, and heightened risk of burnout.

Empathetic listener: It describes a person with a proactive approach when it comes to understanding and acknowledging the emotions, concerns, and experiences of others. They give undivided attention, validate feelings, and offer support without judgment.

Extraversion: It refers to an active orientation toward the external world, where individuals derive energy from social interactions and external stimuli. Extraverts tend to be outgoing, talkative, and enthusiastic, actively seeking the company of others.

FOMO (Fear of Missing Out): This refers to the anxiety or unease caused by the fear of not being involved in or missing out on enjoyable or exciting experiences or opportunities.

Generation Alpha: The generation born after Generation Z, usually starting from the mid-2010s onward.

Generation X: The generation born between the mid-1960s and early 1980s, often thought of as reliable, adaptable, and independent.

Generation Y: Also known as Millennials, this generation typically refers to individuals born between the early 1980s and late 1990s.

Generation Z: The generation born between the mid-1990s and early 2010s, also known as digital natives, who grew up in the era of technology and social media.

Go-getter: A proactive and ambitious individual who actively seeks opportunities, takes the initiative, demonstrates a relentless drive for success, and is willing to go the extra mile to achieve their goals, often exhibiting resilience and determination in the face of challenges.

Hustle culture: A cultural trend that glorifies constant busyness, working long hours, sacrificing personal well-being, and valuing productivity above all else, often leading to chronic stress, burnout, and neglect of self-care.

Impostor syndrome: It's a psychological pattern where individuals doubt their accomplishments, fear being exposed as a fraud, and experience persistent self-doubt, perfectionism, and chronic stress, often leading to burnout and diminished self-esteem.

Information overload: It refers to the overwhelming amount of information available, bombarding individuals with constant data input, resulting in difficulties in processing, and decision-making, decreased productivity, heightened stress levels, and cognitive overload.

Introversion: It refers to a preference for internal reflection and a decreased need for external stimulation. Introverts typically find solitude energizing and may engage in introspection or individual activities to recharge.

Job crafting: It highlights the proactive process of employees reshaping their job roles and responsibilities to better align with their skills, interests, and values, with the aim of reducing burnout and increasing job satisfaction.

Job dissatisfaction: It's about a persistent sense of dissatisfaction or unhappiness with a person's job, stemming from various factors such as unfulfilling tasks, lack of recognition, or poor work-life balance, and if unaddressed, it can lead to chronic stress, burnout, and career stagnation.

Micromanagement: It describes the excessive control or monitoring of an employee's work, stifling autonomy, undermining trust, increasing stress levels, and resulting in burnout and decreased job satisfaction.

MBTI (Myers-Briggs Type Indicator): It's a widely used personality assessment tool based on the theories of Carl Jung. It categorizes individuals into sixteen distinct personality types based on their preferences. Its goal is to provide insights into a person's natural inclinations and preferences.

Perfectionism: It's the tendency to set extremely high standards for oneself, engage in excessive self-criticism, and relentlessly pursue unattainable goals, ultimately contributing to burnout, anxiety, and diminished well-being.

Pomodoro Technique: It refers to a time management method that involves breaking tasks into focused intervals, usually 25 minutes long, separated by short breaks, in order to enhance productivity and maintain focus.

Presenteeism: It describes the practice of being physically present at work but being unproductive, disengaged, and mentally exhausted due to burnout, health issues, or other factors impacting work performance and well-being.

Psychological capital: It refers to positive psychological resources, including self-efficacy, optimism, resilience, and hope, which can act as protective factors against burnout and enhance well-being in the workplace.

Purpose-driven work: It refers to the pursuit of meaningful and fulfilling work aligned with personal values and passions.

Quiet quitting: It acknowledges the act of talented employees leaving a job or organization without providing clear communication or feedback about their intentions or reasons for departure.

Remote work fatigue: Exhaustion and weariness experienced by individuals working remotely for an extended period, often due to factors like increased screen time, blurred work-life boundaries, and limited social interaction.

Snowflakes: A term used to describe individuals from younger generations, often Generation Z and Millennials, who are perceived as overly sensitive, easily offended, and lacking resilience in the face of challenges and criticism.

The aggregation of marginal gains: The practice of making small, incremental improvements in multiple areas that, when combined, lead to significant overall improvement.

Time blocking: Time blocking is a scheduling technique where specific blocks of time are dedicated to specific tasks or activities, helping individuals prioritize and manage their time effectively by assigning specific time slots for different activities.

Toxic productivity: It points out a harmful mindset that glorifies relentless work and constant productivity without considering the negative consequences on physical and mental well-being.

Ultradian rhythms: These are recurring biological cycles shorter than 24 hours that influence various bodily functions, such as sleep stages, hormone release, and cognitive performance.

Work-life imbalance: It's an imbalance between work and personal life where work demands and responsibilities overshadow personal time and well-being.

Work-life integration: It refers to a more flexible approach to work-life balance that seeks to blend and integrate work and personal life harmoniously and aims to reduce burnout and enhance well-being.

Work martyrdom: The belief that constantly sacrificing personal time, well-being, and self-care for work is necessary or admirable.

Workaholism: It highlights an addictive need to work excessively and compulsively, often at the expense of personal well-being, relationships, and overall life satisfaction.

YOLO (You Only Live Once): It's a popular acronym and philosophy emphasizing the importance of living life to the fullest, embracing new experiences, taking risks, and prioritizing enjoyment and fulfillment in the present moment without excessive concern for the future or long-term consequences.

Zoom exhaustion: It refers to fatigue, mental strain, and burnout resulting from excessive use of video conferencing platforms, such as Zoom, due to remote work or virtual meetings.

REFERENCES

A quote from Susan Cain. (n.d.). Goodreads. https://www.goodreads.com/quotes/9096131-when-your-conscientiousness-impels-you-to-take-on-more-than

Al Dilby, H. K., & Farmanesh, P. (2023). Exploring the impact of virtual leadership on job satisfaction in the post-COVID-19 era: The mediating role of work-life balance and trust in leaders. *Frontiers in Psychology, 14.* https://doi.org/10.3389/fpsyg.2023.994539

Alaoui, S. (2021, May 5). *Pandemic builds solidarity around urgency of mental health.* United Nations Foundation. https://unfoundation.org/blog/post/pandemic-builds-solidarity-around-urgency-of-mental-health/

Ali, A. (2022, April 21). *Conductor gives employees YOLO months for work-life flexibility.* Allwork.Space. https://allwork.space/2022/04/conductor-gives-employees-yolo-months-for-work-life-flexibility/

Attard, M. (2022, July 26). *Communicating for engagement against rising burnout.* Forbes. https://www.forbes.com/sites/forbesagencycouncil/2022/07/26/communicating-for-engagement-against-rising-burnout

Berman, R. (2022, August 18). *Exercise for muscle strength: How often, not how much you do it may be key.* Medical News Today. https://www.medicalnewstoday.com/articles/exercise-for-muscle-strength-how-often-not-how-much-you-do-it-may-be-key

Bullock, B. G. (2017, August 14). *How mindfulness beats job stress and burnout.* Mindful. https://www.mindful.org/mindfulness-beats-job-stress-burnout/

Cain, S. (2012). *Quiet: The power of introverts in a world that can't stop talking.* Crown Publishing Group.

Ciampi, R. C. (2019, December 6). *Stress and burnout.* Psychology Today. https://www.psychologytoday.com/us/blog/when-call-therapist/201912/stress-and-burnout

Cross, R., Singer, J., & Dillon, K. (2020, July 9). *Don't let micro-stresses burn you out.* Harvard Business Review. https://hbr.org/2020/07/dont-let-micro-stresses-burn-you-out

De Knoop, J. (2023, February 15). *The power of taking breaks: Why it's essential for career development for professionals and business owners.* LinkedIn. https://www.linkedin.com/pulse/power-taking-breaks-why-its-essential-career-business-de-knoop/

Deloitte. (2018). *Burnout survey.* https://www2.deloitte.com/content/dam/Deloitte/us/Documents/about-deloitte/us-about-deloitte-burnout-survey-infographic.pdf

Edith Cowan University. (2022, August 15). *Exercise answer: Research shows it's how often you do it, not how much: We all know exercise is important, but is it better to do a little every day, or a lot a few times a week?* ScienceDaily. https://www.sciencedaily.com/releases/2022/08/220815085707.htm

Employee burnout: Causes, signs, and strategies. (2021, June 15). Personio. https://www.personio.com/hr-lexicon/burnout/

Flynn, J. (2023, March 30). *20+ alarming burnout statistics [2023]: Stress and lack of motivation in the workplace.* Zippia. https://www.zippia.com/advice/burnout-statistics/

Foods to help with burnout and emotional stress. (n.d.). Titanic Spa. https://www.titanicspa.com/blog/foods-help-burnout-emotional-stress

Gabriel, K. P, & Aguinis, H. (2022). How to prevent and combat employee burnout and create healthier workplaces during crises and beyond. *Business Horizons, 65*(2). 183-192. https://doi.org/10.1016/j.bushor.2021.02.037

Gao, X., Ma, K.-L., Wang, H., Gao, Q., Lei, L.-J., & Wang, T. (2019). Association of sleep quality with job burnout among Chinese coal mine staff: A propensity score weighting analysis. *Scientific Reports, 9,* 8737. https://doi.org/10.1038/s41598-019-45329-2

Gleeson, J. R. (2022, March 17). *Sleep deprivation or burnout?* Michigan Medicine. https://www.michiganmedicine.org/health-lab/sleep-deprivation-or-burnout

Grabowski, S. (2021, September 26). *How to manage burnout with mindfulness.* The Mindful Steward. https://themindfulsteward.com/how-to-manage-burnout-with-mindfulness/

Green, A. A., & Kinchen, E. V. (2021). The effects of mindfulness meditation on stress and burnout in nurses. *Journal of Holistic Nursing, 39*(4), 356-368. https://doi.org/10.1177/08980101211015818

Health benefits to meal planning. (2021, March 13). Community Health Collaborative. https://chtc.sites.uiowa.edu/news/2021/03/health-benefits-meal-planning

Horvat, M., & Tement, S. (2020). Self-reported cognitive difficulties and cognitive functioning in relation to emotional exhaustion: Evidence from two studies. *Stress and Health, 36*(3), 350–364. https://doi.org/10.1002/smi.2930

How ignoring workers' mental health hurts your workplace. (2021, May 6). Ranstad. https://www.randstad.ca/workplace-insights/corporate-culture/consequences-ignoring-workplace-mental-health/

How to combat burnout with mindfulness meditation. (n.d.). ProjectX. https://www.projectxfactor.com/post/combat-burnout-with-mindfulness

Huffington, A. (2014). *Thrive: The third metric to redefining success and creating a life of well-being, wisdom, and wonder.* Harmony/Rodale.

Jarm, I. (2021, February 25). *How sleep can prevent burnout.* LinkedIn. https://www.linkedin.com/pulse/how-sleep-can-prevent-burnout-iva-jarm/

Khan, T., Komm, A., Maor, D., & Pollner, F. (2021, June 4). *"Back to human": Why HR leaders want to focus on people again.* McKinsey & Company. https://www.mckinsey.com/capabilities/people-and-organizational-performance/our-insights/back-to-human-why-hr-leaders-want-to-focus-on-people-again

Kipman, U., Eibl, S., Bartholdy, S., Weiß, M., Schiepek, G., & Aichhorn, W. (2021). Personality traits among burnout patients: Differences between psychiatric burnout patients and controls with regard to the big 5 personality traits. *International Journal of Clinical Studies & Medical Case Reports.* https://doi.org/10.46998/IJCMCR.2021.14.000326

Kirby, R. (2022). *The Sparkle: How to beat burnout, end exhaustion and find a career that lights you up.* Sparklehouse Press.

Klein, A., Taieb, O., Xavier, S., Baubet, T., & Reyre, A. (2020). The benefits of mindfulness-based interventions on burnout among health professionals: A systematic review. *EXPLORE, 16*(1). 35-43/ https://doi.org/10.1016/j.explore.2019.09.002

LaMotte, S. (2022, March 10). *Burnout may be changing your brain. Here's what to do.* CNN. https://edition.cnn.com/2022/03/10/health/burnout-changing-brain-wellness/index.html

Levitt, M. D, (2020, September 13). *How ignoring burnout in your company will cost you in the long run.* LinkedIn. https://www.linkedin.com/pulse/how-ignoring-burnout-your-company-cost-you-long-run-michael-levitt/

Maida, J. (2022, April 27). *Creators of Take Our Daughters to Work day reveal why*

boys weren't originally included. Yahoo Life. https://www.yahoo.com/life
style/the-history-of-take-our-daughters-to-work-day-130654900.html

Marks, L. (2022, November 21). *Everything you need to know about workload
management.* Runn. https://www.runn.io/blog/workload-management

Maslach, C., & Leiter, M. P. (2016). Understanding the burnout experience:
Recent research and its implications for psychiatry. *World Psychiatry, 15*(2),
103–111. https://www.ncbi.nlm.nih.gov/pmc/articles/PMC4911781/

Matyanowski, M. (n.d.). *Beyond the buzzwords: Demystifying the 16 personality
types.* MatchBuilt. https://matchbuilt.com/blog/16-personality-types/

Mayer, M. (2012, April 13). *How to avoid burnout: Marissa Mayer.* Bloomberg.
https://www.bloomberg.com/news/articles/2012-04-12/how-to-avoid-
burnout-marissa-mayer

Mayo Clinic. (2021). *Job burnout: How to spot it and take action.* Mayo Clinic.
https://www.mayoclinic.org/healthy-lifestyle/adult-health/in-depth/
burnout/art-20046642

Mazur, C. (2023, February 11). *40+ worrisome workplace stress statistics [2023]:
Facts, causes, and trends.* Zippia. https://www.zippia.com/advice/work
place-stress-statistics/

Michael, J. (2017, December 26). *Pause: 15 Quotes On Why You Should Take
Breaks, Relax, And Play.* Bplans Blog. https://articles.bplans.com/pause-
quotes-take-breaks-relax-play/

Mijanou. (2023, January 28). *The importance of disconnecting during breaks: How
to recharge and refocus for maximum productivity.* Smunch. https://www.
smunch.co/en/blog/the-importance-of-disconnecting-during-breaks-
how-to-recharge-and-refocus-for-maximum-productivity

Mindset Development Group. (2022, September 15). *The magic of marginal
gains theory: Sweat the small stuff.* https://www.mindsetdevgroup.com/
blog/marginal-gains-theory/

Molade, O. (2021, May 4). *Combating burnout with nutrition.* Nutritionist
Resource. https://www.nutritionist-resource.org.uk/memberarticles/
combating-burnout-with-nutrition

Montañez, R. (2019, August 18). *3 essential tactics for conquering sleep deprivation
and burnout.* Forbes. https://www.forbes.com/sites/rachelmontanez/
2019/08/18/3-essential-tactics-for-conquering-sleep-deprivation-and-
burnout/

Moore, C. (2019, December 30). *Resilience theory: A summary of the research*

(*+PDF*). PositivePsychology.com. https://positivepsychology.com/resilience-theory/

Muscaritoli, M. (2021). The impact of nutrients on mental health and well-being: Insights from the literature. *Frontiers in Nutrition, 8.* https://doi.org/10.3389/fnut.2021.656290

Nazish, N. (2020, February 28). *How to make time for exercise—even when you're super busy.* Forbes. https://www.forbes.com/sites/nomanazish/2020/02/28/how-to-make-time-for-exercise-even-when-youre-super-busy/

Norton, N. (2013). *The power of starting something stupid: How to crush fear, make dreams happen, and live without regret.* Shadow Mountain.

Pacheco, D., & Rehman, A. (2022, April 14). *How is sleep quality calculated?* Sleep Foundation. https://www.sleepfoundation.org/sleep-hygiene/how-is-sleep-quality-calculated

Penttinen, M. A., Virtanen, J., Laaksonen, M., Erkkola, M., Vepsäläinen, H., Kautiainen, H., & Korhonen, P. (2021). The association between healthy diet and burnout symptoms among Finnish municipal employees. *Nutrients, 13*(7), 2393. https://doi.org/10.3390/nu13072393

Pivot. (2023, February 21). *What ignoring employee burnout could mean for your business.* https://pivot.co/blog/ignoring-employee-burnout

Poudel, K. (2022, August 22). *14 tips on how not to burnout at work.* Dev Ops. https://thedevpost.com/blog/how-not-to-burnout-at-work/

Prakash, P. (2023, February 13). *"Bare Minimum Monday" is the latest workplace trend hitting productivity.* Fortune. https://fortune.com/2023/02/13/bare-minimum-monday-is-the-latest-workplace-trend-hitting-productivity/

Preventing burnout—the importance of vacation time. (n.d.). Homewood Health. https://homewoodhealth.com/corporate/blog/preventing-burnout-the-importance-of-vacation-time

Psycherg. (2021, April 20). *What is the cost of ignoring your employees' emotional wellness to your organisation?* https://www.psychreg.org/cost-ignoring-employee-emotional-wellness/

Rameer, V. M. (n.d.). *40+ statistics on burnout in the workplace you can't ignore.* Science of People. https://www.scienceofpeople.com/burnout-statistics/

Rise Science Editorial Team. (n.d.). *Burnout is preventable, but you'll have to rethink how you work and sleep.* Rise. https://www.risescience.com/blog/sleep-loss-burnout-sales

Roberts, C. (2020, February 16). How to set boundaries at work to avoid burnout. CNET. https://www.cnet.com/health/how-to-set-healthy-boundaries-at-work-to-avoid-burnout/

Sánchez-Hernández, Ó., Barkavi-Shani, M., & Bermejo, R. M. (2022). Promotion of resilience and emotional self-care in families and health professionals in times of COVID-19. *Frontiers in Psychology, 13*. https://doi.org/10.3389/fpsyg.2022.879846

Sankofa, C. (2022, December 1). *Burnout quotes for powerful regeneration.* Everyday Power. https://everydaypower.com/burnout-quotes/

Scott, E. (2022, March 31). *How to take a break from work (and why you need it).* Verywellmind. https://www.verywellmind.com/why-you-should-take-a-break-3144576

Scott, E. (2020, October 21). *Traits and atitutudes that increase burnout risk.* Verywell Mind. https://www.verywellmind.com/mental-burnout-personality-traits-3144514

Singh, J., Steele, K., & Singh, L. (2021). Combining the best of online and face-to-face learning: Hybrid and blended learning approach for COVID-19, post vaccine, & post-pandemic world. *Journal of Educational Technology Systems, 50*(2). 140–171. https://doi.org/10.1177/00472395211047865

Smith, M. (2022, October 6). *50% of workers are burned out and "productivity paranoia" could be making it worse: "People are just worn down."* CNBC Make It. https://www.cnbc.com/2022/10/06/microsoft-50-percent-of-people-are-burned-out-at-work.html

Tang, R., Friston, K. J., & Tang, Y.-Y. (2020). Brief mindfulness meditation induces gray matter changes in a brain hub. *Neural Plasticity, 2020*, 1–8. https://doi.org/10.1155/2020/8830005

Van Rensburg, G. J. (2023, April 19). *How proper nutrition can help lower stress levels and prevent burnout.* White River Manor. https://www.whiterivermanor.com/news/how-proper-nutrition-can-help-lower-stress-levels-and-prevent-burnout/

Waters, K. (2023, March 3). *Use food as fuel to fight burnout.* BenefitsPRO. https://www.benefitspro.com/2023/03/03/use-food-as-fuel-to-fight-burnout/

Weir, K. (2019, January). *Give me a break.* American Psychological Association https://www.apa.org/monitor/2019/01/break

Wong, K. (2020, November 24). *Burnout: How to identify and avoid it on the job.* Achievers. https://www.achievers.com/blog/burnout-job/

World Health Organization. (2019, May 28). *Burn-out an "occupational*

phenomenon": International classification of diseases. https://www.who.int/
news/item/28-05-2019-burn-out-an-occupational-phenomenon-
international-classification-of-diseases

World Health Organization. (2022, June 8). *Mental disorders.* https://www.
who.int/news-room/fact-sheets/detail/mental-disorders

Zwilling, M. (2022, October 18). *How baby boomers fit in the realm of entrepreneurship.* Advisorpedia. https://www.advisorpedia.com/growth/how-
baby-boomers-fit-in-the-realm-of-entrepreneurship/

www.ingramcontent.com/pod-product-compliance
Lightning Source LLC
Chambersburg PA
CBHW061155120626
46546CB00005B/2079